D1627205

Defending Your Faith

Norman Geisler & Joseph Holden

PUBLISHING GROUP
NASHVILLE, TENNESSEE

© 2002 by Norman Geisler and Joseph Holden
All rights reserved
Printed in the United States of America

ISBN: 978-0-8054-2482-9

Published by B & H Publishing Group
Nashville, Tennessee

Subject Heading: YOUTH/CHRISTIAN LIVING

10 11 12 13 14 15   11 10 09 08 07

Contents

About the Authors

NORMAN L. GEISLER, president and professor of theology and apologetics at Southern Evangelical Seminary, is a leading Christian apologist with more than fifty books to his credit. Among them are *Baker's Encyclopedia of Apologetics, Unshakable Foundations, Answering Islam, When Skeptics Ask, When Critics Ask,* and *When Cultists Ask.*

JOSEPH M. HOLDEN, adjunct faculty member for Faith Seminary, earned his master's degree in apologetics at Southern Evangelical Seminary in Charlotte, North Carolina.

Acknowledgments

This book is affectionately dedicated to our wives, Barbara and Theresa, who have lovingly and patiently supported us through the years. We are especially grateful for their encouragement during the writing of this book.

We want to give special recognition to Brad Adams, who worked diligently on the initial grammatical edits and the creative scenarios in the manuscript to help prepare for the publisher. We are also grateful to Steve Strimple of Santa Fe Christian Upper School and Steve Keels for their helpful suggestions in producing a manuscript that is both practical and meaningful.

Finally, we wish to express our appreciation to those at B&H Publishing Group for believing in this work.

Above all, we are indebted to our Lord, who has given us the ability to exchange ideas about Him and His creation. It is our hope that the reader will be drawn into a closer relationship with Him.

Introduction

For Parents and Teachers

Why a study guide for high school students? Because America's youth are on the front line of the spiritual war between persons who worship God and those who seek to cultivate a world apart from God. Yes, the battle lines are well *beyond* being drawn; the adversary and his minions have launched a multifront offensive against the moral foundation of our country and institutions.

What evidence is there of such a war? Who is winning? The news from the battlefront is not good. Consider the following statistics compiled by William Bennett, the former secretary of education in the Reagan administration.

- SAT scores fell seventy-three points, even though inflation-adjusted expenditures rose more than 200 percent.
- Violent crime was up 550 percent.
- Births to unwed mothers were up 400 percent (and accounted for 30 percent of all births).
- The number of unmarried teenagers who gave birth increased 200 percent (approximately 40 percent of all teenage pregnancies ended in abortion).
- Abortion occurred to 1 out of every 4 pregnancies—nearly 40 million by 1998 (more than 90 percent of all abortions had nothing to do with rape, incest, or the life of the mother).
- Teenage suicide was up 200 percent.
- Divorce was up 125 percent.[1]

All this occurred between 1960 and 1992 while the country's population only increased by 41 percent! Based on these statistics, it's a rout, and our side would appear to be losing ground rapidly.

Don't we have the best equipment in the Word of God? Don't we have the best leader in Jesus? Don't we have the best inspiration in the Holy Spirit? And don't we have the best provider in God, who is all-knowing, all-powerful, always present, and absolutely faithful and good? Of course we do!

Nonetheless, we do not seem able to effectively and resolutely *defend* our faith. We are often unprepared to tackle the tough questions and challenges the opposition aggressively runs at us. Because we fail to put on our armor and equipment, we are bowled over in shame and embarrassment when we cannot offer a reasonable explanation for our faith. We must be able to fend off attacks and go on the offensive to recruit the opposing players to our side. Jesus so commanded in Matthew 28:19–20.

A lack of religious and moral education has left us defenseless without the necessary ammunition to wage the war, to carry the cross. Not surprisingly, Bennett's discouraging data pertains to the same time period the U.S. Supreme Court ruled all of the following are unconstitutional in public schools: devotional prayers (1962), Bible readings (1963), the Ten Commandments (1980), and teaching creation alongside evolution (1987). Under the cry of "separation of church and state," the opposition forcibly removed anything associated with a Judeo-Christian moral education from the public education system. (It is ironic that the curriculum of a traditional *liberal* arts program at one time included religious/moral training.) With confidence, G. Richard Bozarth, an avowed atheist, boldly claimed in the late 1970s, "Finally, it is irresistible—we must ask how we can kill the god of Christianity. We need only insure that our schools teach only secular knowledge. . . . If we could achieve this, God would indeed be shortly due for a funeral service."[2]

The opposition, however, has not been satisfied with simply removing the church or religious/moral teaching from the schools and all other public institutions. It thrust a new "ism," a new set of beliefs called secular humanism, into the moral educational vacuum (1961). Secular humanism contends that we must be tolerant and nonjudgmental of others and their beliefs—not out of a duty to love our neighbor as we love ourselves, but because there is no *abso-*

lute good and bad and, indeed, no moral absolutes whatsoever.[3] The nonbelief in moral absolutes is referred to as moral relativism.

Secular humanism is *secular* in that it contains no reference to God as the moral authority of the universe. Persons who are secular humanists either believe that God never existed, God is dead, or God is alive but irrelevant. The belief system is humanistic not only because it is man-centered (anthropocentric) versus God-centered (theocentric), but also because it assumes the essential goodness and the theoretical perfectability of humanity. Secular humanism does not proclaim that man is good in an absolute sense (after all, there are no absolutes), but human character and behavior are improvable through the concerted efforts of man (the individual) and society. Therefore, progress can be made and the human condition can improve without God's help or guidance. Lost somewhere and somehow is the human sin nature.

We know we all are human beings, and yet we each are unique. Secular humanism focuses on the uniqueness of each individual and crops out all that human beings have in common. Thus, because each of us is a unique moral agent, secular humanism argues that we have individualized moral codes that are unrelated to a universal standard. As a consequence, I may like or dislike, to varying degrees, your moral code in relation to my moral code, but I cannot claim to have the authority to condemn your moral code because there are no moral absolutes. All I can say is your moral code is not for me or that you have not behaved consistently with your individualized moral precepts.

Denying that moral absolutes exist (i.e., moral relativism) has impacted every cultural segment and institutional component of American society. The collective conscience of the nation has all but atomized into millions of self-conscious opinions and tastes, and these "preferences" constitute an ever-changing and amorphous moral constellation that lacks definition, grading, and dimension.

Is it any wonder that good thoughts are now denigrated and bad thoughts are promoted? If nobody's wrong because everybody's right, all thoughts and actions are of equivalent moral value. Just think of it: Adolf Hitler and Mother Teresa made of the same moral fiber?

It's easy to see how the removal of Judeo-Christian moral education and the rise of secular humanism/moral relativism have affected our schools. Note the following comparison of classroom problems in the 1940s and 1990s, according to surveyed public school teachers and as formulated by William Bennett:[4]

1940s	1990s
talking	drug abuse
chewing gum	alcohol abuse
making noise	pregnancy
running in halls	suicide
cutting in line	rape
improper clothing	robbery
littering	assault

What can be done? What *must* be done? As educator J. P. Moreland has said, "The church must train high school students for the intellectual life they will encounter at college."[5] Research shows that a significant percentage of teens claim to be Christians but hold beliefs that are inconsistent with the Bible. Researcher George Barna said of the teens in a recent survey, "Among teenagers, what we see is what we will continue to get from them—well-intentioned but misinformed faith perspectives that lead to bad choices and spiritual confusion. As the future leaders of the Christian church, we must be concerned about the substance of the faith that will be communicated and be practiced in the long-term."[6] Let's hope they have not become spiritual casualties, only wounded and not eternally lost. Carl Henry, the theologian, further states, "Unless evangelicals prod young people to disciplined thinking, they waste—even undermine—one of Christianity's most precious resources."[7]

This book is written for the purpose of preparing, training, and arming high school students for the morally relativistic, even anti-Christian, world they will encounter upon entering college or the workplace. By no means will that world be totally new to them, but it may become overpowering once they are in it full time. As parents and teachers, it is our duty to do our utmost to assure that our young adults are armed and well equipped for the battle that will ensue.

The battle of ideas is the battle for the minds of the next generation. As we win minds, we can win hearts with the Holy Spirit's intervention. A mind and heart won can lead to a family won, which can lead to a neighborhood won, which can lead to a community won, which can lead to a state won, which can lead to recapturing our nation for the glorification of God. This study guide is intended to be refreshing and educational. We have tried to write in a conversational, dialogue-like style that avoids the use of esoteric, twenty-five-cent words. Stuffy, academic language has its place but not here where we are attempting to fashion a door that permits relatively easy and broad access to the field of Christian apologetics.

Welcome and come in. You are encouraged to invite your students to read, mark, think, question, and debate (optimally in this order). If this book lifts your students' ability to defend the faith or makes them thirst for further study and/or helps them present the gospel message to others, it will have served a worthy purpose in our ongoing spiritual battle and defense of our faith.

For Students

Before we address the most important questions about Christianity, it seems best to outline our goals and approach. This study guide approaches apologetics in a step-by-step manner. It contains thirteen chapters that build upon one another. Chapters 1 and 2 introduce the field of apologetics and explain *why* we need to learn it. Chapters 3 through 12 are part of a three-step process that demonstrates the truthfulness of Christianity. Chapter 13 concludes the book with helpful advice for when an authority figure challenges your faith in the classroom. The overall "process" is structured to discuss the topics of each chapter in logical order. The objective is to familiarize you with the needed steps in reaching others with the gospel message (see 1 Corinthians 15:1–10). The first two steps in the process will encompass chapters 3 through 8. These chapters are dedicated to strengthening you in the Christian worldview and to offer answers to those perspectives that challenge the foundations of Christianity (Psalm 11:3). It is believed that a worldview is the framework or lens by which one understands and interprets the facts. Once the Christian worldview has been established, people can correctly interpret the evidence offered in chapters 9 through 12.

The titles at the beginning of each chapter are in question format and represent the most-often-asked questions among high school and college students. Each chapter begins with a story scenario and a few questions that are intended to help you discuss what you think about the chapter's main topics *before* you read the chapter. The idea is to encourage you to reflect on what you think, why you think what you do, and who or what has had a major influence on your thinking. In addition, each chapter will provide you with an overview of what you will be learning. This will prepare you for what information is to follow.

At the end of each of the thirteen chapters are review questions that will help you measure how much information you retained from your reading. Each question will help you focus your study on the main points of each chapter and can be used for class discussion. After you read the entire chapter and answer the review questions at the end, go back to the beginning of the chapter and attempt to answer the questions after the scenario. In what ways would you now change your answers? Has your understanding increased?

Most apologetic books approach defending Christianity primarily as an academic discipline. In this guide, every effort is made to view learning apologetics as a necessary foundation for surviving the anti-Christian environment often experienced on university campuses and in the workplace. Being prepared will enable you to become a skillful evangelist and defender of God's Word. That is to say, you are learning to defend the faith to better understand God's Word and to give reasons to those who ask about or object to Christianity. Even if a college education is not planned anytime soon, the benefits of learning how to defend God's Word at your workplace or with friends are indispensable. Our ultimate goal is not only to equip you before entering college but to help you enjoy learning about one of the most interesting topics known to man: God.

The following outlines our overall goals and approach.

Goals

- To familiarize you with the study of apologetics
- To equip you to defend your faith and evangelize others (1 Peter 3:15; Matthew 28:19–20; Acts 1:8)
- To help you gain an appreciation for the uniqueness of Christianity
- To prepare you, the student, to interact with others about various topics at the college level

Approach

- To approach learning apologetics not only as an intellectual exercise but as a tool for impacting others for Christ
- To show you, the student, *what* you must learn and *why*
- To provide encouragement for further study
- To teach topics that are necessary for the moment, leaving the more complicated for later

CHAPTER 1
What Is Apologetics?

Scenario

In Surfer's Paradise, California, high school seniors Peter and Jordan have just finished their first PE class of the fall semester. Jordan transferred into the school and knows no one. Their lockers are next to each other.

Peter: Whew! It's hot out there. I'm totally drained.

Jordan: Yeah. . . . I'm Jordan.

Peter: Peter.

Jordan: Are they going to make us run that many laps every day?

Peter: Maybe. I can't wait to get home and get in the water.

Jordan: You surf?

Peter: As much as I can. You?

Jordan: Born to ride, man!

Peter: How about some surfing later?

Jordan: Have to pass. It's my sister's birthday. Got to do the family routine. But I always go Sunday morning; it's my spiritual trip for the weekend, right? Work for you?

Peter: No can do. I go to worship service at 9:00 Sunday morning, and—

Jordan: No way!

Peter: Way. And then I've got my high school group from 10:00 to 12:00. We also meet on Wednesday nights—you know,

Bible study and some basketball. So, how about we get together Sunday afternoon for some waves if the water is nice?

Jordan: I'm surprised. You actually believe in God, Jesus, the Bible, and all that stuff? I thought, you know, you were too cool.

Peter: Uhhh . . .

Questions

- How would you respond if you were Peter?
- Is it cool or not cool to believe in God?
- Do you feel embarrassed, uncomfortable, or defensive in openly proclaiming your beliefs to a nonbeliever?

Purpose

To describe and define Christian apologetics

Goal

To gain an understanding of Christian apologetics and its limitations

In this chapter you will learn

- that the word *apologetics* refers to defending the Christian point of view.
- that apologetics has positive and negative sides.
- that evidential, historical, classical, and presuppositional are the four major approaches to apologetics.
- that the power of apologetics is limited and can't in itself make anyone a Christian.
- that when doing apologetics you should follow certain fundamental guidelines.

The word *apologetics* should not scare you. It's not a disease, nor is it a Christian who is "sorry" for his or her faith in Jesus Christ. The English word *apologetics* comes from the Greek word *apologia,* which literally means a "reasoned defense." In other words, apologetics is the branch of Christian theology that attempts to give answers to persons who ask questions about or object to Christianity.

An apologist presents various evidences to defend his or her faith. Apologetics is not presented in Scripture as an *optional* task, only for some special group or person to engage in; rather, it is a *command* for all Christians. The Bible says that we should be able to give an answer to anyone who asks about and questions our faith. The apostle Peter writes, "But sanctify the Lord God in your hearts, and always be ready to give a defense to everyone who asks you a reason for the hope that is in you, with meekness and fear" (1 Peter 3:15).

Things you should know about apologetics

- The word *apologetics* is not a military word; it is a word that describes how a lawyer gives a verbal defense for a client in the courtroom before a judge and jury. That is, it tells how apologetics should and should not be done. This means we don't beat on people by clobbering them with our Bibles but by speaking gently and humbly to them.

- The Greek form of the word *apologia* is used at least nine times in the New Testament (see 1 Corinthians 9:3; 2 Corinthians 7:11; 1 Peter 3:15; Philippians 1:7, 17; 2 Timothy 4:16; Acts 19:33; 22:1; 25:16). This word can be traced back to the fourth century B.C. when the Greek philosopher Plato used it to title one of his books, *Apology*. His book gives the account of Socrates's (Plato's teacher) defense before a court of law that charged him with corrupting the youth of Athens and leading them into atheism.

- Apologetics is not new. It is something we do every day, even sometimes without knowing. It's simply giving "reasons" or "evidences" for why we believe something to be true.

- Apologetics has positive and negative sides. The positive side of apologetics is when we give reasons for why Christianity is true. Unlike the negative side, which tears down objections, we can build up confidence in Christ by providing good reasons, archaeological and scientific evidence, or some other available tools.

  The positive use of apologetics is seen in Acts 1:3, when after rising from the dead Jesus showed Himself with many "infallible proofs": "He also presented Himself alive after His suffering by many infallible proofs, being seen by them during forty days and speaking of the things pertaining to the kingdom of God."

Jesus also did positive apologetics for His disciples when He gave them evidence of His bodily resurrection in Luke 24:38–40: "And He said to them, 'Why are you troubled? And why do doubts arise in your hearts? Behold My hands and My feet, that it is I Myself. Handle Me and see, for a spirit does not have flesh and bones as you see I have.' When He had said this, He showed them His hands and His feet."

God did positive apologetics in Romans 1:19–20 by giving evidence of His existence through the created world: "What may be known of God is manifest in them, for God has shown it to them. For since the creation of the world His invisible attributes are clearly seen, being understood by the things that are made, even His eternal power and Godhead, so that they are without excuse."

The negative side evaluates reasons offered against Christianity and exposes their weaknesses. In other words, the negative side of apologetics makes it its task to "tear down" or "dismantle" ideas that are given to discredit Christianity. When "tearing down" reasons, it is crucial to accomplish this by refutation not condemnation. Don't get involved in tearing down anyone. Refuting a person's claims against Christianity is simply giving *reasons* for why we think the claims are false. If we begin raising our tone of voice and getting angry at the person we are talking to, we are entering the area of condemnation.

An example of a biblical command to engage in the negative side of apologetics is 2 Corinthians 10:4–5: "For the weapons of our warfare are not carnal but mighty in God for pulling down strongholds, casting down arguments and every high thing that exalts itself against the knowledge of God, bringing every thought into captivity to the obedience of Christ."

Now that you know the difference between both the positive and negative side of apologetics, turn to the following Scriptures and try to discover which side of apologetics is being used: 1 Kings 18; Exodus 4:1–9; 2 Corinthians 10:4–5.

Are there different kinds of apologetics?

There are different ways to build a defense for your faith. Each of the following apologetic types has a different *starting* place when attempting to answer persons who ask about Christianity. These types often overlap and use one another's methods of showing Christianity to be true. Although there are more than four types of apologetics, these seem to be the most popular.[1]

1. *Evidential apologetics* focuses primarily on providing evidences that people can see with their own eyes. These apologists give evidence consisting of ancient copies of the original Bible (also called manuscripts), archaeological discoveries, or even scientific truths that are consistent with Scripture. The evidential apologist would say, "Look at the *facts with your own eyes*. This will prove the truthfulness of Christianity."

2. *Historical apologetics* focuses primarily on providing historical evidences. These apologists give evidences that are gathered from old historians such as Suetonius, Tacitus, and Josephus. Their purpose is to show that the Bible is historically accurate. The historical apologist would say, "Look to the *past* to support the truthfulness of Christianity."

3. *Presuppositional apologetics* defends Christianity from certain basic assumptions. The presuppositional apologist assumes the truth of Christianity without using traditional proofs for the existence of God. One basic presupposition the apologist holds is that non-Christians have presuppositions that obscure or taint everything they hear about God. It is the apologist's role to present the truth of Christianity and the falsehood of any worldview opposed to Christ. Unlike classical apologetics, which begins with reasons and evidence, presuppositionalists begin by assuming the Christian worldview and by attempting to show that only it makes sense out of the world.[2] The presuppositional apologist asserts that "proofs for the existence of God are unnecessary; simply state the truthfulness of Christianity and show the weaknesses of other worldviews."

4. *Classical apologetics* focuses primarily on providing well-reasoned answers to persons who ask about or object to the Christian religion. Classical apologists begin by establishing the reality of absolute truth and proceed to show evidence for the existence of God and the possibility of miracles. Then they proceed to show historical evidence that supports the deity of Christ by examining His sinless and miraculous life, fulfillment of prophecy, and His resurrection from the dead. However, they usually begin by giving reasons apart from showing physical evidences in order to change the unbeliever's perspective (also

called a *worldview*) on life and religion. When this is accomplished, they can accurately assess and interpret the physical evidence. The classical apologist says, "Change their worldview since it's the reason why unbelievers misinterpret the facts they see with their eyes. Once this is accomplished, show them the historical evidence." (See the "Apologetic Goal" and diagram on pp. 24–25 for the topics addressed by classical apologetists.)

What are the limits of apologetics?

It is important to remember that apologetics is limited and can't in itself make anyone a Christian. However, it can help clear the ground for anyone to receive Jesus Christ by removing obstacles that hinder saving faith. Just as a plow clears away snow from an icy road so cars can pass unhindered, apologetics clears away questions and doubts so the gospel can shine through to the unbeliever.

The limitations of apologetics also can be understood this way: it can only bring the horse to the water, so to speak; the horse is the only one who can decide to drink. It is the same way with salvation. Apologetics can show an unbeliever that Jesus is the Water of life, but the decision to drink is made by the unbeliever. This is the difference between "faith that" and "faith in."

Apologetics helps an unbeliever to see *that* Jesus is the way to salvation, but it is the role of the Holy Spirit and the individual as to whether he will place faith *in* Jesus. Apologetics can demonstrate *that* Jesus is the way to heaven by providing evidence; however, faith in Jesus can only be achieved through a personal decision apart from apologetics. In other words, apologetics goes only so far. Limitations, however, don't lessen the role that apologetics plays in bringing someone closer to Christ. After all, the unbeliever cannot believe *in* God until he first believes *that* God exists (Hebrews 11:6).

The following illustrates the *limits* of apologetics.

Faith *that* God exists	Faith *in* God
Is an area of apologetics	Is an area of evangelism
Addresses the mind	Addresses the will
Uses reasons and evidence	Requires the Holy Spirit
Comes before faith *in*	Comes after faith *that*
Points the person *to* Jesus	Places trust *in* Jesus[3]

What are the rules of a good apologist?

To ensure good results, remember the following rules when using apologetics. They will help you become more effective when talking to others about Christianity. We have tried to make them easy to remember by placing them into the acronym A.P.O.L.O.G.E.T.I.C.S.

A = Always pray
P = Pre-evangelism (establishing a theistic worldview)
O = Obstacles are to be removed
L = Love your neighbor
O = Overcome discouragement
G = Gospel message given
E = Encourage friendships
T = Truth
I = Illuminate and illustrate
C = Christ centered
S = Scripture use

Congratulations! You have just finished your first chapter in apologetics. The purpose of this section was to describe and define Christian apologetics—a foundation for the second chapter. Now that you know *what* apologetics is, you can learn *why* it is important. Before you continue, test how much you remember by completing the following chapter review questions.

Review

1. The word *apologetics* literally means _____

_____

2. The word *apologia* is used at least _____ times in the New Testament.
3. There are two sides to apologetics: a _____ side and a _____ side.
4. Apologetics is the branch of Christian theology that _____

_____

_____

_____

_____.

5. Name the four different apologetics systems, and list each branch's primary focus.

(1) _____

_____

(2) _____

_____

(3) _____

_____

(4) _____

_____

6. In a few sentences, describe the difference between "faith that" and "faith in." Which one does apologetics directly address?

_____

_____

_____

_____

_____

_____

_____

7. List the rules of a good apologist.

_____

_____

_____

_____

_____

_____

_____

_____

_____

_____

CHAPTER 2

Why Apologetics?

Scenario

Jordan drives over to Peter's house on the beach about 1:00 on Sunday afternoon. As is common for an early fall afternoon, the wind is changing its direction. This gives the guys only about half an hour before the ocean surface becomes too choppy. They wait for another set of waves.

Peter: The wind picked up real fast, but it was pretty good there for awhile.

Jordan: Yeah, it was great. I'm feeling better all the time about my dad getting transferred here. Up there, we didn't have any waves except in the winter.

Peter: Don't you miss your friends?

Jordan: Yea, kinda. I mean, a lot of them got into drugs and stopped surfing. I tried some stuff, but I'm addicted to surfing. This ocean is my playground. This is where I come to have some fun.

Peter: You're a good surfer, not just ripping waves with radical maneuvers.

Jordan: Thanks . . . and this wave is mine.

Jordan returns.

Peter: Great ride! Thank God He made the ocean with awesome waves.

Jordan: God? Why do you believe in someone you cannot see, touch, or hear? It doesn't seem rational to me.

Peter: Well . . .

Questions

- Why does Peter have to explain anything?
- Do you think Peter can explain his faith in a way that Jordan will understand?
- Do you try to explain your faith to nonbelieving friends, or do you try to avoid the topic?

Purpose

To convey the need for Christian apologetics

Goal

To understand why Christian apologetics is both necessary and biblical

In this chapter you will learn

- that the Bible commands us Christians to do apologetics.
- that several biblical characters used apologetics.
- that it is unreasonable to believe without evidence.
- there is a need to give an answer to persons who ask why we believe the Christian worldview.

We hope you enjoyed learning the basics of apologetics. If you are in the fog about chapter 1, don't worry; as you continue you will look back and understand it more clearly.

By way of review, chapter 1 dealt with *what* apologetics *is*, its different kinds of approaches, its limits, and, finally, the rules that help guide a good apologist. However, chapter 2 will build on this foundation by discussing *why* Christians should *do* apologetics. There are several good reasons why, but perhaps the most important of all is that the Bible tells us to.

The Bible commands us to do apologetics

1 Peter 3:15–16: "But in your hearts reverence Christ as Lord. Always be prepared to make a defense to any one who calls you to account for the hope that is in you, yet do it with gentleness and reverence; and keep your conscience clear, so that, when you are abused, those who revile your good behavior in Christ may be put to shame" (RSV).

Jude 3: "I found it necessary to write appealing to you to contend for the faith which was once for all delivered to the saints" (RSV).

Philippians 1:7, 16: "For you are all partakers with me of grace, both in my imprisonment and in the defense and confirmation of the gospel . . . knowing that I am put here for the defense of the gospel" (RSV).

2 Timothy 2:24–25: "And the Lord's servant must not be quarrelsome but kindly to every one, an apt teacher, forbearing, correcting his opponents with gentleness. God may perhaps grant that they will repent and come to know the truth, and they may escape from the snare of the devil" (RSV).

Titus 1:9: "Holding fast the faithful word as he has been taught, that he may be able, by sound doctrine, both to exhort and convict those who contradict."

God did apologetics

- God gave Moses evidence that He was speaking through him (Exodus 4:1–9).
- God raised Jesus from the dead to prove He is the Son of God (Romans 1:4; John 2:18–22).
- God used apologetics through Elijah as he proved that God was more powerful than Baal was (1 Kings 18:37–39).

Jesus did apologetics

- Jesus gave evidence of His resurrection to His disciples by showing His pierced hands and feet (Luke 24:39–40).
- Jesus showed Himself alive after His resurrection by many "infallible proofs" (Acts 1:3).
- Jesus said He would rise from the dead to give evidence to the Jews that He had authority to cleanse the temple (John 2:18–21).
- Jesus provided evidence by physically healing a crippled man to prove He had the authority and power to forgive sins (Mark 2:8–11).

- Jesus gave evidence to Thomas that He was indeed alive and well after His resurrection (John 20:26–29) by showing His crucifixion scars.
- Peter said Jesus was confirmed by God through the miracles He had done in the presence of witnesses (Acts 2:22).
- Jesus offered His miracles as proof to those who were sent by John the Baptist to ask if Jesus was really the Christ (Matthew 11:5).

The apostle Paul did apologetics

- Paul continued to prove to the Jews in Damascus that Jesus was the Christ (Acts 9:22).
- Paul's custom was to enter the synagogues in a given city and reason, explain, demonstrate, and persuade anyone who would listen to believe in Christ (Acts 17:2–4; 18:4, 19; 19:8).
- Paul gave reasons to believe in Christ to the philosophers in Athens (Acts 17:22–34).
- Paul showed evidence through various signs that he was an apostle (2 Corinthians 12:12).
- Paul gave a defense of his ministry before an angry crowd in Jerusalem (Acts 22:1).

It is unreasonable to believe without evidence

Reasons are crucial when trying to decide what to believe. If we have beliefs that are not supported with evidence or good reasons, they're called "unreasonable beliefs." Hopefully, few of these exist in our belief systems.

Many people see no reason to believe Christianity. This is where apologetics can make a difference—namely, by offering good reasons to believe. After all, would we place our trust in an airplane or a bus if we didn't have good reason to believe that it could take us on our journey? Probably not. Nor would we put our trust in a chair before having good reason to believe that it would support our full weight.

Then why do we expect people to place their trust in Jesus if they don't have good reasons to believe that He can save them? None of us became Christians because it is unreasonable. Actually, it was the opposite; we committed ourselves to Christ because it is the reasonable thing to do (Romans 12:1–4).

There is a need to give an answer

Already this century much is being said about Christianity; however, not everything is good. For many of us it is hard to understand why anyone would speak out against Christ. Nevertheless, for various reasons, many objections cut deep into the heart of our faith. For example, some persons cast doubt on God's existence, Christ's resurrection, forgiveness of sins, and the trustworthiness of the Bible, all of which comprise the foundation of the historic Christian faith. *The fact of the matter is plain: if these doubts are confirmed to be true, then Christianity is false.* The apostle Paul told of the dark consequences when he wrote to the Corinthian church:

> But if there is no resurrection of the dead, then Christ is not risen. And if Christ is not risen, then our preaching is empty and your faith is also empty. Yes, and we are found false witnesses of God, because we have testified of God that He raised up Christ, whom He did not raise up—if in fact the dead do not rise. For if the dead do not rise, then Christ is not risen. And if Christ is not risen, your faith is futile; you are still in your sins! Then also those who have fallen asleep in Christ have perished. If in this life only we have hope in Christ, we are of all men the most pitiable. (1 Corinthians 15:13–19)

The consequences Paul speaks of paint a gloomy picture if the objections raised by unbelievers are true. We should not fear, however, because they can be viewed as opportunities to share good reasons why we trust in Christ. There are two very good reasons why we Christians should give answers to unbelievers:

1. The Bible commands us to "be ready" to give an answer "always" (1 Peter 3:15–16; Jude 3; Titus 1:9) to anyone who asks about our faith in Christ. As discussed previously, this means that doing apologetics is not simply an option that *some* people choose; it's God's command to *all* Christians. We may never come across anyone who asks the hard questions about our faith, but Peter says we should be prepared just in case.

2. Unbelievers have good questions and we have good answers (Colossians 4:6). Because Christianity is true, the evidence will always be on our side. The key is to investigate and search out the evidence. In other words, the answers are there; it's only a matter of finding them.

Remember, whenever we give good answers to unbelievers, we are removing one more obstacle that stands in the way of their receiving Christ. Keep in mind, the answers we give are not given simply for making ourselves look smart. The ultimate goal is to create an atmosphere in which the unbelievers might come to the knowledge of the truth. We can create this atmosphere by providing answers that remove many of the unbelievers' questions and doubts (John 14:1–11; Luke 24:38–43).[1]

The following diagram illustrates how apologetics goes before evangelism (if necessary) to clear the ground for an unbeliever to see the gospel clearly. Once the obstacles have been removed, the gospel can penetrate through the barrier and be understood without being corrupted, distorted, or changed by the unbeliever's worldview.

The proper role of apologetics

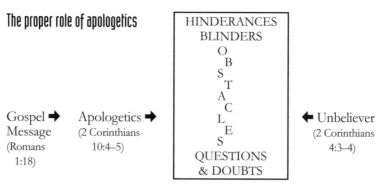

Review

1. How does the theme of chapter 2 differ from chapter 1?

_____

_____

_____

_____

_____

2. Give four reasons why Christians should do apologetics?

(1) _____

(2) _____

(3) _____

(4) _____

3. List two verses as examples of Jesus removing the disciples' doubts and hindrances with good reasons and evidence.

(1) _____

(2) _____

4. Why do beliefs need to have good reasons to support them?

_____

_____

_____

_____

_____

5. List at least three consequences if Christianity is not true.

(1) _____

(2) _____

(3) _____

6. List some of the hindrances that may stand between the gospel message and the unbeliever? _____

_____

_____

_____

7. What is the ultimate goal in giving an answer for our faith?

_____

_____

_____

_____

_____

The Apologetic Goal

Our "apologetic goal" is to *establish the truthfulness of Christianity*. To accomplish this, certain topics need to be addressed in logical order. For example, before we show the Word of God to be trustworthy, we must first demonstrate that there is a God who can give a Word. It makes no sense to speak the truth about Jesus and His miracles unless truth first exists and can be known.

So, to achieve our goal, the foundation of truth must be laid first. This is because we intend to make truth statements about God and Christianity. Someone who doesn't believe that truth exists will not believe us when we claim that Christianity is "true" (John 14:6; 17:17). After truth is established, we can make truth statements about God's existence. Miracles, the Word of God, the Son of God, and the Resurrection can be defended once God's existence is established. If what we say about these topics is true, then it follows that Christianity must also be true. The following diagram will show the three-step process in which we will demonstrate Christianity to be true. It will also serve as the study guide outline for the remainder of the book.

CONCLUSION: Christianity Is True!

STEP 3: Evidential (tangible) Apologetics
Is the Bible the Word of God?
Did Jesus Rise from the Dead?
Is Jesus God?
Can the Bible Be Trusted?

STEP 2: Theistic (God) Apologetics
Are Miracles Possible?
If God Exists, Why Evil?
What about Other Worldviews?
What about Evolution?
Does God Exist?

STEP 1: Philosophical (reason) Apologetics*
What Is Truth?

*Chart adapted from Professor Richard Howe's unpublished class notes, Southern Evangelical Seminary, 1996.

CHAPTER 3
What Is Truth?

Scenario

After getting out of the water, Peter and Jordan dash to Peter's house to take hot showers. Later, they mix two fruit smoothies and sit down in front of the big window in the living room.

Jordan: Peter, you told me in the water that you believe God is the Creator of all things and that Jesus is the Way.

Peter: Yea, that's what I believe.

Jordan: Where did you get that?

Peter: Easy. Common sense and the Bible.

Jordan: I'm not knocking it, but I'm kinda confused. People I know believe all kinds of things.

Peter: Like karma and past lives. Oh, yea, how about channeling? Whoa!

Jordan: But, Peter, how about all that mystical stuff about Jesus being fully God and fully human at the same time and being raised from the dead? That's pretty unbelievable too.

Peter: It's not the same because it's true.

Jordan: You mean you *believe* it to be true.

Peter: You could put it that way, but what I'm trying to tell you is that I'm so convinced it's true that I know it's true.

Jordan: Wow. . . . I guess what is true depends on who is saying what is true. But is there any way of proving what is true,

or is it just a matter of opinion? You know what I mean?
What is truth?

Peter: Uhhh . . .

Questions

- How should Peter respond to Jordan's last question, "What is truth?"
- How do you know something is true or false?
- Why is it important to know what is true about the natural world, human relationships, and God?

Purpose

To define and understand the nature of truth

Goal

To learn how to define a biblical perspective of truth and how to respond to the views of truth that challenge Christianity claims

In this chapter you will learn

- that truth is important because of its crucial foundational nature in establishing the Christian *worldview*.
- the "correspondence theory" of truth: Truth is telling it like it is.
- that numerous biblical examples support the correspondence theory.
- that other definitions of truth are inadequate or self-defeating.
- the four barriers to truth: agnosticism, skepticism, relativism, and subjectivism.

The first two chapters laid the groundwork for asking a series of questions about Christianity. Now that we know giving answers for our faith is not an option but rather a biblical command, we can turn our attention to the *first step* in our apologetic goal: the question of the nature of "truth." Truth should be addressed first because the remainder of the questions we will ask about Christianity requires true answers. That is, unless truth is real, it would make no sense to offer true answers about the Christian faith.

Why is truth important?

Beyond what has already been said, there are at least two other good reasons for why truth is important.

1. A personal relationship with truth in the bodily form of Jesus Christ is impossible unless we believe that truth is real and discoverable. Jesus said, "I am the way, the *truth,* and the life. No one comes to the Father except through Me" (John 14:6, italics added). If we cannot recognize the truth, how are we going to recognize Jesus who *is* Truth?

2. Truth is *foundational.* Unless truth is real, how are we going to tell "the truth" about Christianity, God, and His Son? Each of us would be left to his or her own story about Christianity. And if everyone has a different story about Jesus, how can we tell which story to believe? In other words, unless truth is real and recognizable, no true Christianity exists, only different stories about it. This means that an unbeliever's story about Jesus would have the same value or weight as a Christian's story because there would be no way to discover which story is true and which is false. Christianity would be likened to a myth or fable. However, this is not what the apostle Peter said in 2 Peter 1:16: "For we did not follow cunningly devised fables when we made known to you the power and coming of our Lord Jesus Christ, but were eyewitnesses of His majesty."

What is truth?

The answer to "What is truth?" is surprisingly easy. Truth is *telling it like it is.*[1] That is, our statements about something must match the real facts as they actually are in the world. Statements have "truth value"; they can be either true or false. By applying the meaning of the statement to the facts as they exist helps us discover true-or-false value. This process of discovering truth asks whether someone's words match what really happened.

For instance, if we were to declare, "Jesus rose from the dead," we would try to discover the statement's truthfulness by searching out and investigating the facts and evidence surrounding Jesus' resurrection. In short, we would have to review the eyewitness reports, look at the archaeological findings, and check to see whether the tomb was empty. If the facts support the above statement, it would be considered a truth. This is the same way our court system attempts to discover the truth. Just remember, truth is simply telling it like it really is, and, by contrast, a lie is deliberately telling it like it isn't!

The following will help make clear the process of discovering truth:

Statements *match* facts and evidence = Truth

Statements *do not match* facts and evidence = Falsehood or lie

Remember, a distinction between our statements and the facts as they are in the real world must exist or else there could be no way of discovering which statements are true and which are false. The fancy name for this definition of truth is the "correspondence theory" because truth *corresponds* or *relates* to reality (the real world) as it actually is.

Biblical examples of the correspondence theory

- Joseph said to his brothers, "Send one of you, and let him bring your brother; and you shall be kept in prison, that your words may be tested to see whether there is any truth in you" (Genesis 42:16).
- Ananias and Sapphira lied by misrepresenting their finances to the apostles (Acts 5:1–4). The couple did not tell the facts as they corresponded to reality.
- How can we tell who was telling the truth when God said, "You shall surely die" (Genesis 2:17) and Satan said, "You will not surely die" (Genesis 3:4)? Satan was the liar because what he said did not correspond to reality. Adam and Eve did eventually die—first spiritually, then physically.
- The ninth commandment is predicated on the correspondence theory of truth. "You shall not give false testimony against your neighbor" (Exodus 20:16 NIV).
- Nebuchadnezzar wanted to know the facts as they *corresponded* to his real dream (Daniel 2:9).
- Other passages are Acts 24:8, 11; 1 Kings 22:16–22; and Proverbs 14:25.[2]

The correspondence view of truth provides something outside the statement itself as a positive test, namely *reality*. Reality can be the ground by which all truth claims—whether Muslim, Buddhist, Hindu, Mormon, Christian, or Atheist—are tested.

Is truth what works?

Some people say that truth is found in whatever works or brings the best results. This view poses several problems. First, it confuses what truth *does* with what truth *is*. Just because a statement may help us gain our intended result does not make that statement true. Although truth does work (the way God intends it to), what works is not always true. For example, lying may work for us; however, this does not make the lie true. It still misrepresents the facts. There is no such thing as a "true lie." It's contradictory. Truth cannot contradict itself, and as Christians we are to avoid contradictions (1 Timothy 6:20).

Suppose you are a star witness in a big court case. Do you think the judge will allow you to tell "what works and nothing but what works, so help you God"? Of course not! The judge wants "the truth and nothing but the truth." Truth must match the facts as they really exist.

Is truth found in good intentions?

According to this view, truth is found in what we *intend* to say instead of what we *actually* say. For example, if I give you directions to get to my house and I tell you to turn left at Broadway Street when I really *intended* to tell you to turn right at Broadway, the directions I gave you would be considered correct according to the intentional-ist. This view of truth fails for several reasons.

1. It mistakenly focuses on what we intend to say rather than on what we actually say. Truth is not found in what we *don't* say; rather, it is found in what we *do* say. This is so because we can't read another person's mind. The only way we can know what others are intending is by what they say.

2. If this view is true, there could never be a sincere, well-intending person who is wrong. If truth is found in good intentions, we would have to conclude that the well-intending atheist is telling the truth about God's nonexistence! How about the well-intending Jehovah's Witness or Mormon who comes to our front doors? Do their good intentions make their doctrines true? What if a student placed the wrong answer on the test sheet but had every intention of marking the right answer? Should the teacher give full credit for the wrong answer? Of course not. Yet if truth were found in good

intentions, we would have to answer each of the above questions with a yes.

3. The Old Testament considers certain *unintentional* acts wrong, therefore requiring a sacrifice (Leviticus 4:2–10, 27).

4. Lies can have good intentions, however this does not make a lie true (remember, a true lie is a contradiction).[3]

Is truth a matter of perspective?

The perspective view of truth is perhaps the most popular. It says that truth is a matter to be decided by the individual. For example, in our scenario with Peter and Jordan, the perspective view of truth would say that a statement could be true for Peter but not necessarily for Jordan. In fact, Jordan essentially said, "All truth is a matter of one's perspective." There are at least two problems here.

1. Jordan's statement boomerangs and destroys itself because the statement would apply equally to the rest of the people on earth. That is, we would merely have to respond by asking, "Is that the truth, or is that only your perspective?" If Jordan's statement is true for all people, then he defeated his original statement, which Jordan says is only his perspective, leaving open the possibility that truth is discovered by another way. Statements similar to Jordan's also boomerang and destroy themselves. Try to develop an eye for these kinds of statements by using the "boomerang principal" to detect the error in reasoning in the following statements:

- Never say the word *never.*
- I can't speak any words in English.
- Language doesn't have meaning.
- Absolutely no truths exist that apply to everyone.

2. If something is true, it is true for *all people,* at *all times,* and in *all places* regardless of a person's awareness or beliefs. For example, if it is true that George Washington was the first president of the United States, then it would be true for everybody in all places and at all times. If something is true, it extends to all regardless of the person's perspective or religious beliefs. Two plus two equals four for everyone everywhere!

What are the barriers to truth?

Now that we know what truth is—namely *that which corresponds to reality* or *telling it like it is*—we can look at some of the views that challenge the Christian position. Let's review and respond to the four most formidable barriers to truth.

Nobody can discover truth

This first barrier claims that truth can't be known, nor can anyone have knowledge of God. This belief is known as "agnosticism." In 1869 Thomas Henry Huxley coined the word *agnostic*. Huxley was a close friend of Charles Darwin's (1809–82). According to agnosticism, ultimate truth and God can't possibly be known. The very meaning of agnosticism can be found by looking at the word itself. *A* is an alfa-negative that means "no" or "not," and *gnostic* comes from the Greek word *gnosis,* which means "known." Literally, the word means "no knowledge" or "no truth."

Even though agnosticism has different forms, it is the hard-and-strict form that concerns us. If truth can't be known, how can we know anything about God or the Bible, which claim to be the truth (John 17:17)? Christianity would be on the same level as mythology, fables, folklore, and fantasy, and we Christians would be left with mere speculation concerning our faith.

Many philosophers and theologians have pointed out several flaws with agnosticism.

1. *When examined more closely, agnosticism self-destructs.* An agnostic (a person who believes in agnosticism) fails to see that he does indeed *know* something about God: he knows that he can't know God. If agnosticism were true, he would not be able to make any statement that contains knowledge about God, including his agnostic one.

2. *The very assertion that "humans can't know truth" is a truth statement in itself.* If an agnostic can't know truth, then how does he or she know agnosticism is true? In other words, the agnostic uses truth to say there is no truth! The boomerang principle strikes again.

3. *When the agnostic makes a negative statement asserting he "can't know about truth or God," he presupposes knowledge about truth and God.* Remember, every negative claim presupposes positive knowledge. For example, a negative statement by a person who says, "The shirt is not white," assumes he knows something about what the shirt color actually is or he could not be sure it is not white. In the same way, agnosticism must have some knowledge about God to say that he can't know Him, else how would he know?

Doubt everything that claims to be true

The second barrier to truth is "skepticism," the belief that we should doubt everything, including the truth about Christianity. "Just be skeptical about everything," the skeptic says. It is the philosophy of uncertainty. This radical view of truth is not new. Its roots are deeply planted in ancient times before Christ. In modern times, David Hume (1711–76) was its major champion.

Because of its emphasis on "indecisiveness," this view is particularly threatening to Christianity. Christ calls us to make a decision about Him—either for or against Him—and the world we live in. Skepticism says, "Hold off on that decision and set it aside." Yet, there are several reasons that support rejecting skepticism.

1. *Skepticism self-destructs, as did agnosticism.* It is impossible to be skeptical about *everything*. To do so, we would have to be skeptical about our own skepticism.

2. *To "hold off" on making a decision about the world is actually making a decision about the world.* Many persons fail to see that making no decision is indeed a decision. If we were to apply skepticism to a real-life situation, we would quickly discover that it is self-destructive. For example, if your car were stopped on railroad tracks with an oncoming train one hundred feet away, would it be wise not to make a decision? If no decision is made to move the car forward or backward, you have actually made the decision to stay in harm's way.

3. *Jesus combated skepticism in His own ministry.* After physically rising from the dead, He addressed His disciples' doubts by offering His pierced hands and feet for examination (Luke 24:38–39). Jesus further reduced their skepticism by eating a piece of broiled fish with them (Luke 24:42).

Truth is different for everyone; it's "relative"

The third barrier to truth makes it a matter of one's own perspective. This view is called "relativism." It denies that truth is absolute and that it applies to *all people* in *all places* and at *all times*.

Relativism, and its many forms, is by far the most popular view of truth on university campuses today. Professor Allan Bloom says in his book *The Closing of the American Mind*, "There is one thing a professor can be absolutely sure of: almost every student entering the university believes, or says he believes, that truth is relative."[4]

There are at least three different kinds of relativism: (1) Truth is relative to time. In other words, what was true *then* is not necessarily true *now*. (2) Truth is relative to persons. That is, whatever is true for *you* is not always true for *others*. (3) Truth depends on location. Meaning, what's true in China may not be true in the United States.

Relativism is the most common barrier to the Christian view of truth—that truth corresponds or relates to reality (correspondence theory). Relativism has become so accepted among high school and college students that Christians who believe that truth is "absolute" are considered closed-minded, exclusive, and intolerant.

There are several reasons for rejecting relativism.

1. As were agnosticism and skepticism, relativism is self-destructive. The statement "all truth is relative" *is* an absolute truth statement. Remember, the relativist is saying that his statement is true for all people in all times and in all places. If it is true for all people in all times and in all places, it is an "absolute" truth!

In reality, relativism is impossible. To affirm relativism, a person must use an absolute truth. Further, to get to the heart of the matter, ask the relativist if his view of truth is only his perspective, or is it true for all people in all times and in all places? If it is just his perspective, it leaves the door open for the possibility of absolute truth to exist since his statement is self-contained and applies only to his own limited perspective. Alternatively, if he says his view is true for all people in all times and in all places, he is no longer a relativist but unknowingly believes in absolute truth.

2. If truth is relative to something else, what is it relative to? It can't be relative to the relative to the relative, and so forth. That is to say, truth must have something fixed and absolute by which to correspond in the real world. If there is nothing in the real world for a person's view of relativism to correspond to, there is no test to see whether it is true.

Some college professors try to prove relativism by facing their students and saying, "The clock on the wall is on my right side," but it is on the left side of the onlooking students. It appears as if the professor proves his point that truth is relative since the clock is on his *right* but on the students' *left*.

However, the professor failed to realize that there are *two* different statements hidden within this illustration. One statement refers to the location of the clock from *the professor's* perspective (facing the class), and the other statement refers to the clock from the student's perspective (facing the professor). Therefore, two separate statements must be evaluated from each perspective. Each statement contains truth-value that is unique only to its own statement. It is clear that the professor's statement that the clock is on his right side is an absolute truth for everyone in the class. However, it is a different question when asking what side the clock is on from the onlooking students' perspective. It is an absolute truth for everyone, including the professor, that the clock is on the students' left side.

All truth is absolute. The statement 2 + 2 = 4 is not only true for mathematicians and professors; it is true for all people everywhere and of every religious and philosophical persuasion.

Truth is what feels right

The fourth barrier to truth is "subjectivism"—the belief that feelings, emotions, and intuition are the keys to discovering what is true. To put it plainly, truth is what *feels* right. The idea behind this view is that truth *feels good* and error *feels bad*. Many Mormons have erred when they appeal to the "burning in the bosom" feeling as a test of whether the Book of Mormon is true. Subjectivism contains several flaws.

1. *Feelings are a poor test for what is true because feelings and emotions change.* Changing feelings can't be used as a basis for the unchanging truth; otherwise, truth could change right along with our feelings. Just think of the implications. The law of gravity would have to be revised daily depending on which scientists *felt* it was true. Encyclopedias that contain historical truths would have to be altered to reflect the current feelings and emotions of the editor.

2. *What if two people had different feelings about the same statement?* Which feeling should we accept? How do we find out whether the statement is true? Feelings are good, and God wants us to experience and use our feelings and emotions. However, there are proper and improper ways of using feelings. It is proper to use feelings while expressing, sharing, and holding truth, but it's improper to use feelings to prove, test, and support truth.

3. *It is obvious that bad news can be true.* But if only what feels good is true, we would have to reject all news that makes us feel unpleasant. Just think of the implications! When the dentist tells you that

a root canal is needed or when your teacher informs you of a less-than-satisfying grade on the exam, if we dismiss the unpleasant information as lies, we put ourselves in jeopardy of loosing teeth and flunking classes. In short, feelings can be a *result of* or *reaction to* truth, not a *basis of* truth.

Are those who believe in absolute truth intolerant and narrow-minded?

The most frequent charges marshaled against Christians in light of their belief in absolute truth and morality are *intolerance* and *narrow-mindedness*. The picture some wish to paint of Christians is that of a horse with blinders on its eyes, limiting its vision of the world; or that of an ostrich with its head buried in the sand, completely oblivious to the surrounding environment. This attitude, however, is misdirected for several reasons.

First, truth is narrow by definition. If something is true, then its opposite *must* be false. For example, if Peter says his car is totally red, and it's true, then all other statements claiming that Peter's car is white, black, or yellow must be false. No other answer presenting another color could be true. What about math teachers who only accept one true answer on the exam? Are they narrow-minded also? No.

Second, the one making the statement that "absolute truth is too narrow" is in fact giving an absolute truth. If this is the case, then the one making the statement is equally narrow-minded.

Third, those charging Christians with *intolerance* because of holding to absolute truth are confused about the meaning of the word *intolerance*. Intolerance refers to the manner or attitude in which one holds truth, not to the truth itself. In other words, this claim confuses *what* one holds (truth) with *how* he holds it (attitude). If holding to absolute truth makes someone intolerant, then the one making the truth claim of Christian intolerance is equally intolerant.

Fourth, to be labeled as intolerant simply because you disagree with someone is mistaken. To be "tolerant" of other views implies that there is a real *disagreement* between viewpoints. Nobody tolerates what he or she already agrees with. That is to say, the people who charge intolerance because of a simple disagreement really want you to acknowledge and accept what you disagree with under the disguise of "tolerance."

Conclusion

Job well done! You have just finished the first question in step 1 of the apologetic goal. Now that you know the basics of truth and how to respond to its barriers, complete your review, quickly review chapters 1 and 2, and notice how much easier it is for you to understand.

Review

1. Why does the subject of "truth" come in the beginning of this study manual? _____

_____
_____
_____
_____

2. Give two reasons why truth is important.

(1) _____

_____
_____
_____
_____
_____

(2) _____

_____
_____
_____
_____

3. What is truth? _____

_____
_____
_____
_____

4. Truth statements must correspond to: (choose one answer)
   a. good intentions
   b. one's perspective
   c. the facts in the real world
   d. feelings

5. Explain the "boomerang principle." _____

_____

_____

_____

_____

_____

6. Which of the following statements boomerangs on itself?
   a. I am the only tired baseball player.
   b. The subject of truth is very interesting.
   c. There is no truth.
   d. A truth cannot be a lie.

CHAPTER 4

Does God Exist?

Scenario

Peter and Jordan go to Peter's bedroom to find a couple of books that his Bible study group has read during the past year. Peter shows Jordan the sections that discussed how someone discovers what is true and what is not. After they get refills for their smoothies, they climb back into the overstuffed chairs in the living room, which is now bathed in the hot orange light of a glorious sunset.

Peter:	So, truth boils down to just telling it like it is. What you say to be true must match the facts of the real world.
Jordan:	I can agree with that. Wow! Look at the sunset. Now that's awesome!
Peter:	That's true!
Jordan:	But, Peter, how do you know it's true that God exists? I've never talked to Him. I haven't seen Him. Have you?
Peter:	Are you looking at the sunset? Do you see what I see?

Questions

- How do you know that God exists?
- Should you believe in someone you can't see?
- How do you respond to someone who says he doesn't believe in God?

Purpose

To introduce reasons that support the Christian belief in the existence of God

Goal

To learn three crucial proofs that can be used to demonstrate the existence of God to unbelievers

In this chapter you will learn

- that we Christians have good reasons to believe in the existence of God based on the first cause, design, and moral proofs.
- that the *first cause proof* uses the universe to show that God is its cause.
- that the *design proof* uses order in our world to demonstrate that an intelligent designer is responsible.
- that the *moral proof* uses the moral law written in our hearts to show that a moral lawgiver exists.

Philosophers, theologians, and scientists have long wrestled with the age-old question of God's existence. For us, this question is of the utmost importance because all other Christian doctrines flow from God. God's existence is foundational in that Christianity stands or falls on this question. If God does not exist, then He can't possibly have a Son (Jesus). If God does not exist, He can't possibly have given us His Word (the Bible) or performed acts (miracles). Ultimately, success in establishing the Christian perspective lies within our ability through the Holy Spirit to convince unbelievers of the reality of an intellectual, powerful, and good God.

In the second step (theistic apologetics) of our apologetic goal, we will focus our attention on the first question: Does God exist? The answer to this question comes from three proofs—proofs that draw upon evidence from the *origin* of the universe, the *order* we see in the world, and the God-given *standard* of right and wrong that is in each one of us.

Why not use Bible verses alone to show that God exists?

The Bible is the best way to learn more about God and His plan of salvation for humankind. However, not everyone believes that the

Bible is true and reliable. This is why we need other methods to convince someone God exists. When witnessing we should always *start* by using Scripture, but when objections to the Bible arise, we should be ready to use and appeal to proofs that do not come directly from the Bible but are consistent with it.

These proofs can be scientific, historical, or simply common sense. Some examples of this in the Bible can be found in Acts 14:5–18 when Paul and Barnabas used "nature" (v. 17) as a witnessing tool to the unbelievers in Lystra. Also, in Acts 17:22–34, Paul used "poetry" (v. 28) to convince unbelievers in Athens.

Paul seemed to have different ways to witness to different people depending on their spiritual condition. If an unbeliever was religious, perhaps following Judaism, Paul would use the Old Testament Scriptures to convince him that Jesus was the Messiah (Acts 17:1–4). Whenever we witness, the main point is this: the message of the gospel cannot change; however, how we present it can change.

How do we know God exists?

We can be confident and rest assured that God's existence is supported by good reasons and an abundance of evidence. It can be said that no archaeological, historical, or philosophical evidence has ever been conclusively shown to contradict Christianity. In fact, the opposite can be demonstrated. Although many pieces of evidence prove the existence of God, we will focus on three memorizable proofs: the *first cause, design,* and *moral.* All three proofs have a different starting point but the same goal: to demonstrate the existence of the God of the Bible.

The first-cause proof: God must be the first cause of the world.

How did the universe get here? Did it always exist? Was it put here by someone or something else? The first-cause proof seeks to show that *the universe is not eternal,* nor could it have arrived here under its own power. In other words, someone or something must have caused it to exist (Genesis 1:1). The logic behind the proof can be stated in three memorizable statements.

1. Whatever had a beginning had a cause.
2. The universe had a beginning.
3. Therefore, the universe had a cause.

Let's look at each sentence and summarize why we believe each of them to be true.

Whatever had a beginning had a cause. Things don't come into existence by themselves. They must be caused by something. In science the law to define this concept is called the "principle of causality." It says that every effect must have a cause. We see effects in everyday life, such as buildings, watches, paintings, and cars. All of these had a beginning and, therefore, need a cause. Can you think of anything that popped up from absolutely nothing? It has been said, "From nothing comes nothing." You see, the beginning must start somewhere with a first cause.

The natural thought that comes to mind is, *If everything needs a cause, then so does God.* Remember, though, only things that had a beginning need a cause. God is eternal and uncreated and doesn't need a cause. If this were not so, we would have to search for God's cause— and so on and so on into infinity, never reaching the beginning.

If this is true, there must be a cause in the past that doesn't need a cause. This uncaused cause we call "God."

The first cause of all that exists must be eternal and uncreated in order to have the power to start everything else, including the universe. It may seem obvious to us that buildings, watches, and paintings need a cause, but what about our universe as a whole? How do we know the universe had a beginning?

The universe had a beginning. Several years ago, many scientists believed the universe was eternal, with no beginning. In the twentieth century, however, scientists discovered new information that indicates the universe must have had a beginning.[1]

First, by 1927, astronomer Edwin Hubble shocked the scientific community by discovering the expanding movements of our galaxy and beyond. In other words, Hubble found that galaxies were moving away from us at high speeds. This expansion is similar to a bomb exploding; when it hits the ground, dirt and debris fly outward in all directions. This discovery was called the "expanding universe," and it caused some scientists to change their view from an eternal universe to one that must have had a beginning. Why? Because if you were to reverse the expansion, you would arrive back to a point of beginning beyond which there was nothing.

To understand this, think about a film projector. When watching a movie, click the reverse button and watch it play backward.

Eventually you will arrive at the very beginning of the movie where the screen suddenly shows nothing. This is a picture of what would happen if we were to reverse the expanding universe today. We would arrive at a point in time where nothing exists. This gives us good reason to believe the universe must have had a beginning in the distant past.

Second, based on new discoveries similar to the expanding universe, modern scientists are favoring a model of origins called the "big bang theory," which suggests that the universe came into being by a large explosion. Not all of us would agree with all aspects of the theory, but it does suggest a *beginning* to our universe (Genesis 1:1). If the universe had a beginning, it must have had a cause.

Third, another proof that points to a beginning is the wearing down and running out of usable energy. That is to say, our universe is growing old and deteriorating like an old barn or a worn-out pair of blue jeans. Scientists have a law to describe this process: the "second law of thermodynamics."[2] How does this show the universe had a beginning? Think about it. If the universe is unwinding, it must have been wound up at a point in time in the past. Remember the last time you filled the gas tank of an automobile or lawnmower? The more you ran the motor the more gasoline was used. Soon, the needle would indicate the tank was empty. The universe operates in much the same way; namely, running out of usable energy. It could not run out of energy unless it was first filled up in the past. Remember, an infinite amount of energy can't run out any more than an infinite tank of gas. Yet, the universe is running out of energy; thus, it must have had a beginning.

Finally, by the process of elimination, we can discover in which *way* the universe, or anything else for that matter, came to exist. There are only three alternatives. The universe was either:

1. *uncaused.* No, this alternative violates the principle of causality: everything that has a beginning needs a cause of its beginning.

2. *self-caused.* This is impossible because something can't create itself. That is to say, the universe would have to exist prior to it existing. It's like trying to lift yourself off the ground with nothing else to support you.

3. *caused by someone or something else.* Yes! It's the only reasonable explanation. This is the Christian view of how the universe came into existence and is consistent with the principle of causality.

Notice that the first two possibilities of origins either violate the scientific law of causality or are impossible, leaving the only alternative: *the universe must have been caused by someone or something else.* What is more reasonable to believe: the atheist's claim that the universe came into existence from nothing and by nothing, or the Christian's claim that the universe was created from nothing and by someone (Hebrews 11:3)? This someone is called "God." The atheist *does not* have a first cause of the universe; whereas, the Christian does!

Therefore, the universe had a cause. This is the solid conclusion if the two statements of our first-cause proof are true. As we have seen, there is good reason to believe the universe came into being at a certain point in the distant past. And if it had a beginning, it would have had a cause of its beginning because nothing comes into existence on its own. This "cause" we call God.

The design proof

The psalmist said that our created world reveals knowledge about God:

> The heavens declare the glory of God;
> And the firmament shows His handiwork.
> Day unto day utters speech,
> And night unto night reveals knowledge.
> There is no speech nor language
> Where their voice is not heard.
> Their line has gone out through all the earth,
> And their words to the end of the world. (Psalm 19:1–4)

The design proof, which was popularized by William Paley (1743–1805), seeks to show that *design in God's creation points to an ultimate designer (God).* Now that we know there had to be a first cause of the universe, and that it could not have emerged by itself, let's take a look at the second proof for the existence of God. Our goal is to show that the first cause (God) is both *intelligent* and *purposeful.* His intelligence and purpose is found in our universe.[3]

The entire proof can be stated in three sentences.

1. Every design had a designer.
2. The universe has a design.
3. Therefore, the universe had a designer.

Let's look at these statements and show why we believe them to be true.[4]

Every design had a designer. This first statement should be obvious to all. Ordered, intelligent designs such as research papers, speeches, presidential faces sculpted on Mount Rushmore, and computer programs came from the minds of designers. Most of us know from experience that buildings have builders, watches have watchmakers, and paintings have painters. Intelligent design doesn't come together at random any more than *Webster's Dictionary* could be composed by an explosion in a print shop! Design informs us that there is a designer responsible.

The universe has design. Now that we know that design obviously points to a designer, we need to turn our attention to an important question: How do we know the universe is designed? We can answer this question by observing the universe. The design we see is very intricate and complex. For example, a single-cell animal contains the same amount of information as one thousand volumes of the *Encyclopedia Britannica*.[5] Would it be reasonable to assume that an encyclopedia found in the forest had an intelligent cause? Yes! Likewise it would be reasonable to believe that human beings, with all the intelligent brain capabilities, eyeball focusing and inversion abilities, and the complex makeup of the single cell, had an intelligent cause. This obvious complexity within cells has led biochemist Michael Behe to conclude that "the result of these cumulative efforts to investigate the cell—to investigate life at the molecular level—is a loud, clear, piercing cry of 'design!'"[6]

If it is reasonable to believe that computers, cameras, and sophisticated machinery need intelligent causes like humans to create them, why then do some people find it hard to understand the need for an intelligent cause of human existence? After all, the human brain is more sophisticated than the quickest computer, the eyeball more precise and capable than the best camera, and the human hand more flexible and functional than the most advanced robot. With the abundant design in the universe, it is reasonable to believe that a designer is responsible.

Some may say that design is obvious when referring to humans; however, when it comes to the natural world, it is a different story. How does the universe show evidence of intelligent creation?

Many people go about their daily business seemingly blind to the fact that our universe bears marks of intelligent design. However, Paul makes it clear in Romans 1:19–21 that God's design in the universe is "clearly seen" and evident in the things that He has made. Paul proceeds to show that "blindness" to the design found in our universe is a result of "suppress[ing] the truth in unrighteousness" (Romans 1:18).

Astronomer Dr. Hugh Ross lists several pieces of evidence that demonstrate that our world has been intelligently designed to support life. This proof is known as the "anthropic principle" (from the Greek word *anthropos*, meaning human). The following pieces of evidence leave no doubt as to the fine-tuning that is needed to create and sustain an environment suitable for human life. As you read the following extraordinary features of our planet, keep in mind that many evolutionists believe the universe came together by chance. You decide what best explains the question of earth's origin and continued operation: chance or intelligent design.

- If oxygen quantity in the atmosphere were greater than it is now, plants and hydrocarbons would burn up too easily. If it were less, advanced animals would have too little to breathe.
- If seismic activity were greater, too many life-forms would be destroyed. If it were less, nutrients on ocean floors (from river runoff) would not be recycled to the continents through tectonic uplift.
- If the ozone level in the atmosphere were greater, surface temperature would be too low. If it were less, surface temperature would be too high, and there would be too much UV radiation at the surface.
- If the thickness of the earth's crust were greater, too much oxygen would be transferred to or from the atmosphere to the crust. If it were thinner, volcanic and tectonic activity would be too great.
- If Earth's magnetic field were stronger, electromagnetic storms would be too severe. If it were weaker, we would have inadequate protection from hard stellar radiation.
- If Earth's gravitational interaction with a moon were greater, then tidal effects on the oceans, atmosphere, and rotational period would be too severe. If it were less, orbital changes would cause climactic instabilities.

- If Earth's axial tilt were any greater or less, surface temperatures would be too great.
- If carbon dioxide and water vapor levels in the atmosphere were greater, a runaway greenhouse effect would develop. If they were less, the greenhouse effect would be insufficient.
- If Earth's rotational period were longer, diurnal temperature differences would be too great. If it were shorter, atmospheric wind velocities would be too great.
- If the oxygen to nitrogen ratio in the atmosphere were larger, advanced life functions would proceed too quickly. If it were smaller, advanced life function would proceed too slowly.[7]

As evidence of God's handiwork, the natural order of things with the precision and balance of atmospheric and microscopic forces reveal to us the unique design He has left us. Moreover, we have been gifted with intelligent capabilities, which allow us to discover and appreciate not only God's awesome power but also His intelligence. Again, the evidence of intelligent design in our universe points to an ultimate designer, God. He alone is worthy of our praise! (Psalm 19; Romans 1:19–21)

Therefore, the universe had a designer. The above conclusion is true if the first two statements in our design proof are correct. Remember, intelligence gives rise to intelligence. Some people believe that the universe came together simply by natural forces. However, natural forces are never observed producing the kind of specified complexity found in a living cell.

One scientist figured the odds of a one-cell animal to come forth naturally by pure chance at 1 in 10^{40000} (that's a 10 with 40,000 zeros after it!). It takes more faith to believe in this than it does to believe that an intelligent cause created the one-cell animal. Design in the universe points to a great designer. This "designer" we call God.

The moral proof

By way of review, the first-cause proof shows that the universe had a beginning and, therefore, must have had a cause; and the design proof shows that the one who caused the universe must have been intelligent due to the design we discover in the world.

The third and final proof of God's existence will show how a person's ability to know right from wrong in his heart was given by the Creator. The moral proof adds another piece of the puzzle by showing others that God is not only the intelligent cause of the universe, but He is also moral and good. The goal of this proof is to show the unbeliever that if there is a moral law (a standard of right and wrong) in our hearts, then there must be a moral lawgiver, God. Philosophers and theologians of the past discussed this proof with great enthusiasm by analyzing its strengths and weaknesses. When the smoke cleared, it was obvious that the moral proof could stand firmly on its own feet.

The ability to discern right from wrong and to know what one "ought" to do morally is called "moral law"—some call it a conscience. Morals are laws of right and wrong that apply to every person on earth. That is to say, these laws make us aware of how we *should* behave with regard to right and wrong. When we discuss right and wrong actions, we are engaging in the field called "morality" or "ethics." This is why we call this the moral proof.

The entire proof can be stated in three sentences.

1. Every moral law had a moral lawgiver.
2. There is a moral law.
3. Therefore, it had a moral lawgiver.

Let's look at these statements and show why we believe them to be true.

Every moral law had a moral lawgiver. The biblical basis for the moral proof is found in Romans 2:15–16, where Paul writes that humankind "show the work of the law written in their hearts, their conscience also bearing witness, and between themselves their thoughts accusing or else excusing them in the day when God will judge the secrets of men by Jesus Christ." Paul is writing about a moral law that stands in each heart as an internal judge of a person's thoughts and actions.

We know that laws do not emerge on their own; they must be given or legislated. The laws that govern the United States did not appear out of thin air; lawmakers spent countless hours formulating and issuing them to society. Further, medical prescriptions do not get prescribed by themselves; they need prescribers called "doctors." So also does the moral law written within us need a lawgiver. This lawgiver we know as God.

There is an objective moral law binding on all people, everywhere, at all times. How do we know that all humans know the difference between right and wrong? How do we know there is a moral law within us? We can be sure for several reasons.

First, there seems to be an agreement by all people that certain things are *always* wrong. For example, murder, rape, theft, lying, and molestation are held by virtually everyone to be wrong. And everyone desires to be treated with dignity, fairness, and courtesy. If there were no moral law written in the heart, one would expect a wider variety in what people believe to be wrong. This virtually universal agreement by all on what is right and wrong strongly suggests there is a standard within every person's heart.

Second, we find that even those who deny there is any moral order live their lives as though there were. For example, if someone were to stand up in an audience and raise an objection to moral law and we abruptly said, "Who cares what you think? Sit down!" He would be upset for being treated rudely and being denied equal opportunity to speak. It would appear by their words they didn't believe in a standard of right and wrong for all people. However, their reactions to injustice, especially when directed at them, show their true belief in a moral order. It's not necessarily by someone's actions we find out what they truly believe, but by their *reactions*. As soon as they are treated without respect, dignity, or fairness, we discover they truly defend a moral law despite what they might say.

Third, those who deny that there is a standard of right and wrong overlook certain values that should never be denied to anyone. For instance, all people value their own right to disagree, think freely, breathe, eat, live, and exercise free choice. If any of these values were to be denied, we would quickly find out a person's true belief about morals.

Fourth, we often make judgments such as "the world is getting worse" or "better," but these statements are impossible without a standard outside the world for what is "best." The moral law serves as the rule or measuring rod of what is good and bad so that we can judge whether the world is getting better or worse. True progress can't be measured without an ultimate standard by which to measure it.

Therefore, a moral lawgiver exists. It has been shown that moral law does in fact exist within the heart and conscience of humankind. If the first two statements of the moral proof are true, then this conclusion is also true. Just as we need lawmakers who make the laws that govern our country, we need a lawgiver (God) who makes laws governing our thoughts and actions.

Conclusion

Much more could be said concerning these evidences for God's existence. The basic points for each can be easily memorized in three statements. Each proof has a different starting point (universe, design, morals) and a different purpose, and by using all three proofs together, we can show that the God of the Bible indeed exists. This God is intelligent by virtue of His design, powerful as demonstrated by His creative ability, and good due to the moral law written in every person's heart. This intelligent and good Being we call God. If you take the time to familiarize yourself with the proofs, they will become a valuable tool when sharing Christ with others.

Review

1. Why is it important for Christians to be able to give reasons for the existence of God? _____

_____

_____

_____

2. Why are Bible verses not sufficient to prove that God exists?

_____

_____

_____

_____

3. List the names of the three proofs for the existence of God.

_____

_____

4. Describe the main purpose of each proof. _____

_____

_____

_____

_____

5. Why can't the universe be uncaused or self-caused?

_____

_____

_____

_____

6. List a few scientific proofs that the universe had a beginning._____

_____

_____

_____

_____

_____

7. Why is the second law of thermodynamics important when proving the universe had a beginning?_____

_____

_____

_____

_____

CHAPTER 5

What about Evolution?

Scenario

Sarah and Jennifer (Jordan's and Peter's younger sisters) bump into each other as they are leaving their second-period biology class.

Jennifer: Whoops! Sorreeeee!

Sarah: That's OK. I wasn't looking where I was going. I'm new here and kinda anxious to find my way to my next class.

Jennifer: I'm Jennifer (*giggling*).

Sarah: I'm Sarah. Did I say something funny, or is there breakfast stuck in my teeth?

Jennifer: No, no. It was what the teacher said about how we evolved from fish. Sounds like he's spent too much time underwater swimming with the fish. He's got the brain bends or something. Pretty whacked, huh? Maybe that explains why my brother Peter wants to surf all the time. He's just lower on the evolutionary scale than I am!

Sarah: Oh, Peter's your brother? My brother Jordan went surfing with him in front of your house yesterday. Jordan said the conversation was heavier than the waves.

Jennifer: Oh, really?

Sarah: Seriously, Jennifer, don't you think that we could have evolved from simpler life-forms in response to the environment? Sounds logical and scientific to me—although I'm glad I lost those scales along the way!

Jennifer: No way. I've never seen a mermaid except in the movies. Have you?

Sarah: No, but what alternative explanation is there? The garden of Eden and Adam and Eve? Got to go, see ya at lunch?

Questions

- Have you been taught that evolution is the only scientific explanation for the development of life on earth?
- Are you prepared to defend alternative explanations?

Purpose

To define evolution and expose its fragile foundation

Goal

To understand the basic characteristics of evolution and formulate reasons for why Christians believe it to be a false view of the origin and development of life

In this chapter you will learn

- that the two major characteristics of evolution are (1) the belief that first life emerged by chance and (2) the belief that simple life has evolved over millions of years into a more complex state by a process called "natural selection."
- the difference between microevolution and macroevolution.
- that fossil evidence does not support evolution.
- that many expert evolutionists admit their theory has severe problems.
- that the ape-men discoveries were either fakes or not conclusive in proving evolution.
- that public schools can study the evidence for creation without being "religious."
- that the universe shows remarkable signs of intelligent design.

In this section, we turn our attention from answering the tough questions about God's existence to addressing Charles Darwin's theory of evolution. Within public school systems, evolution is often taught as *fact*, while creation is considered a matter of religious *faith*, setting up a perceived conflict between the Bible and science. Today, evolution has penetrated most science classes. This has made evolution a formidable barrier, which hinders many from receiving the Bible's truths.

A Christian student often endures a college professor for an entire semester as he speaks eloquently about how life began by purely natural causes, and never asks a critical question that challenges the basic assumptions of evolutionary theory. However, after finishing this chapter, you will be able to discuss and question evolution with your teachers and fellow students without causing a "holy war" in the classroom. Your insights may prove to be both refreshing and challenging.

Our goal first will be to understand evolution and then to show it to be a false view of the origin of life. Second, we will answer common objections by evolutionists to the Christian doctrine of creation. In answering evolutionists, abundant scientific evidence and good reasons exist apart from using the Bible. These will be helpful in demonstrating that the universe and life were supernaturally created. By avoiding Scripture and using a scientific approach to answer evolution, we will avoid being accused of religious favoritism.[1]

What is evolution?

When talking about evolution, many of us think of Charles Darwin (1809–82) as its founder. Although Darwin may be the most well-known person associated with evolution, its roots go back to certain ancient Greek philosophers. Of greater importance is the evolutionists' central belief that all living things have evolved or developed by purely natural processes from simple forms of life to more sophisticated forms. Various views of evolution have developed; however, the views we will discuss involve the origins of first life and the evolution of new life-forms.

1. Evolutionists believe life began by chance from the right combination of nonliving materials

The first belief concerns the *origins* of first life (known as chemical evolution). According to many evolutionists, a swirl of gases along with water touched by an electrical charge ignited a chemical reaction that generated the building blocks of life.[2] No supernatural element was required; that is, life emerged purely by natural causes. This view directly confronts the biblical model of origins in Genesis 1, where there is an intelligent God that supernaturally created life. Several reasons support why life did not emerge purely by natural causes and from nonliving material.

First, it has been scientifically demonstrated that life never comes from nonlife. We could ask an evolutionist to furnish an example of life emerging from nonliving things, whether observed in nature or in the laboratory without intelligent intervention, but even the pasteurization process has confirmed that life cannot come into existence where there is no life. When Louis Pasteur (1822–95) killed all bacterial life by sterilizing his test tube and placing a seal around the lid, he showed the scientific community that life could not emerge from a nonliving environment.

On the other hand, we Christians can adequately account for the cause of life. God qualifies as the first cause of life because it takes life to give life, and God *is* life (John 14:6; Colossians 1:15–17). Furthermore, what is more reasonable to believe: that life begets life or that nonlife begets life? Have you ever seen a rock bear fruit?

Second, intelligent life needs an intelligent cause. It is unreasonable to believe that intelligent life arose from a nonliving, unintelligent cause. Did the information in *Webster's Dictionary* come together by a gust of wind in a paper mill? No. Were Shakespeare's plays composed by an explosion in a printing shop? No. Did the presidential faces on Mount Rushmore emerge as the result of wind and rain erosion? Of course not! All of these examples were created by an intelligent cause. In other words, it is unreasonable to believe that intelligent life was caused by nonintelligent natural forces.

Third, as discussed previously, the idea that life arose purely by chance is unscientific. Science prides itself on observation and experimentation, not on reasoning based on chance. Besides, the odds of life beginning by chance are very low—and for all practical purposes, zero. Some have calculated the chance to be 1 in $10^{40,000}$. That's more atoms than there are in the universe! It takes more faith to believe in evolution than it does to believe in a supernatural creator.

Fourth, some experts in the field of biology have shown the evolutionary model of the origins of first life (chemical evolution) to be false. Even Darwin himself admitted that "if it could be demonstrated that any complex organ existed, which could not possibly have been formed by numerous, successive, slight modifications, my theory would absolutely break down."[3]

Taking up that challenge, Michael Behe (pronounced Bee-hee), biochemistry professor at Lehigh University, has demonstrated that a living cell shows marks of intelligent design.[4] In his book *Darwin's Black Box,* Behe provides strong evidence that a living cell could not have originated by evolutionary processes because the cell needs all of its parts functioning together at the same time for its survival. This means that the cell could not have come together in stages over long periods of time because it could not have survived with only part of its necessary components intact. With a cell, it's either all or nothing.

Dr. Behe illustrates this point by using a mousetrap.[5] If any one part of the mousetrap is missing or not functioning, it will not work as a whole. It is the same with a living cell. It must have all its parts functioning and in place at one time or it dies. This new discovery challenges evolution by demonstrating that life must have been created fully formed as the Book of Genesis indicates.

2. Evolutionists believe simple life has changed over millions of years into a more complex state by a process of "natural selection"

The second main characteristic of evolution departs from the origins of life (chemical evolution) and addresses the development of *new* life-forms (biological evolution). According to evolutionists, life arose naturally into a one-celled animal, then mutated and changed, or evolved, over millions of years into the various kinds of life we see today—humans being the highest of the chain. This process is said to be guided by what Darwin called "natural selection."[6]

Natural selection is the process by which the weaker species become extinct because they are unable to adapt to changes in their environment. Have you heard the term "survival of the fittest"? According to evolutionists, this process enables the various types to gain biological purity while at the same time weeding out the less fit. The overall effect is said to be an ever more sophisticated and stronger kind.

These different kinds of life, including humans, supposedly share in a common genetic ancestry. This means that in the distant past one kind, such as reptiles, grew into another kind, such as birds. This process continued through the millions of years and finally produced humans. This transition from one kind or type of life into another is called "macroevolution." Changes that occur within the same kind are called "microevolution"; for instance, the various kinds of dogs reflect the reality of microevolution. The following chart will help you distinguish the two types of evolution.[7]

Microevolution	Macroevolution
Change *in* kinds	Change *of* kinds
Change within one *kind* of bird	Change *from* reptile to bird
Possible to occur	*Impossible* to occur
Many fossils to support	*No* fossil support
Does occur today	*Does not* occur today
Can be observed	*Cannot* be observed
Scientific	Unscientific

Christians may accept microevolution ("micro" = small) as a scientific fact. However, when turning to the Book of Genesis, we find a radically different picture of life's development, and that picture is opposed to macroevolution. Moses wrote that God made each individual form of life to reproduce after its own "kind" (Genesis 1:21–26). That is to say, cows give birth to cows, dog to dogs, fish to fish, and humans to humans. No cross-kinds of reproduction or macroevolution occurs.

It is a universal scientific fact that one basic type of life does not give rise to, or transform into, *other* types. There is adaptation *within* a specific kind (for example, some dogs are big and some small, some long hair and some have short hair, etc.) but not a transformation *of* one kind into another (for example, from dog to horse).

Now that you know what evolution is, let's take a deeper look at some of the problems with it.

Problems with evolution

Before we look at the various shortcomings of evolution, remember that it is not necessary to simply quote Bible verses to defeat evolution. Abundant evidence from a scientific and philosophical standpoint shows that evolution should be rejected and creation believed.[8]

First, for evolutionists to establish that over long periods of time one kind of life evolves or changes into a different kind (apes changing to humans, or cats to dogs), they must look initially at the fossil evidence. This is the best way to discover how the various types of life developed throughout time.

If the evolutionists are right, thousands of fossils should have been preserved, showing a transition from one kind into another. For example, we should see fish becoming reptiles and apes changing into humans. This, however, is not what we find. The fossil record is an embarrassment to evolutionists.

The fact of the matter is clear: the fossil record supports creation.[9] Discoveries show that animals appear fully formed and not in "transition," as evolutionists claim. These preserved fossils appear suddenly within the geological column and not spread over long periods of time. This agrees with what Genesis says about the creation in the beginning; namely, that God created all of the animals fully mature and reproducing after their own kind.

Let's look at what some scientific experts in the field are saying about evolution.

- Darwin found it hard to believe that the eye could be formed by natural selection when he asserted, "To suppose the eye with all its inimitable contrivances for adjusting the focus to different distances, for admitting different amounts of light, and for the correction of spherical and chromatic aberration, could have been formed by natural selection, seems, I freely confess, absurd in the highest degree."[10]
- Stephen Jay Gould, professor of geology and paleontology at Harvard University, says, "All paleontologists know that the fossil record contains precious little in the way of intermediate forms; transitions between major groups are characteristically abrupt."[11] Gould goes on to assert, "The extreme rarity of transitional forms in the fossil record persists as the trade secret of paleontology."[12]
- David Raup of the Field Museum of Natural History in Chicago asserts, "We now have a quarter of a million fossil species but the situation hasn't changed much. The record of evolution is still surprisingly jerky and, ironically, we have fewer examples of evolutionary transition than we had in Darwin's time."[13]
- Michael Denton, molecular biologist and medical doctor, says, "As evidence for the existence of natural links between the great divisions of nature, they are only convincing to someone already convinced of the reality of organic evolution."[14]

- Michael Behe, professor of biochemistry at Lehigh University, writes in his book *Darwin's Black Box*, "No one at Harvard University, no one at the National Institutes of Health, no member of the National Academy of Sciences, no Nobel prize winner—no one at all can give a detailed account of how the cilium, or vision, or blood clotting, or any complex biochemical process might have developed in a Darwinian fashion. But we are here. Plants and animals are here. The complex systems are here. All these things got here somehow: if not in a Darwinian fashion, then how?"[15]

Second, systemic changes that occur between different kinds of animals—such as from fish to amphibian or ape to human—must be completed all at once not gradually. The internal system of an animal is such that changes from one kind to another must be immediate or else the animal will die. For example, a person can make minor changes in a car gradually, over time, without altering its basic type. Gradual changes can be made in the shape of the fenders, the car's color, and its trim. But if a change is made in the size of the pistons, this involves *simultaneous* changes in the cam shaft, block, cooling system, engine compartment, and other systems. Otherwise the new system will not function. This is the reason why no fossils support a *gradual* change from one kind of life to another (macroevolution). Although minor changes *within* kinds are possible, gradual changes *of* kinds are not.[16]

Third, different animal types may have similar bodily appearances—such as apes and humans—but this does not automatically make them ancestors, anymore than a bird and an airplane have genetic linkage because of similar body design. Body shape has no necessary connection with common ancestry. Rather, similar body types point to a common Creator that suited animals and humans for a similar living environment.

What about the ape-men discoveries?

Most of us at one time or another have seen science textbooks that feature the pictures of an ape transforming over millions of years into modern man. Occasionally, newspapers print headlines that read, "Ape-Man Discovered!" Why do some scientists seem so eager to believe in ape-men discoveries? Because they are motivated to conclusively show the world that there is a genetic connection between the animal kingdom and human beings. According to evolutionists, such a find would be the crowning proof that would win the war over creationists.

How does the Christian explain these discoveries that seem so authentic? Although it may seem like solid evidence, they usually are nothing more than cases of mistaken identity or pure fantasy. Let's look at some of these "ape-man discoveries" and their shortcomings.

- *Piltdown Man.* This discovery by Charles Dawson in 1912 was said to be evidence of a half-million-year-old ape-man. However, in 1953 it was found out that Piltdown Man was a fake. When the evidence was examined more carefully, scientists discovered that it had been altered to give the appearance of age when actually the jawbone was that of an orangutan.
- *Nebraska Man.* In 1922 a tooth was found on a farm in Nebraska. Initially it was said to be a tooth of a one-million-year-old ape-man. Later, geologist Harold Cook found another tooth, similar to the first one, attached to a skull, which was found to belong to a rare pig.
- *Peking Man.* The evidence for Peking Man has disappeared since 1941. There are serious problems with believing that Peking Man was an ape-man because he died by a blow from a sharp object, which is a highly unlikely cause of death for a prehuman.
- *Java Man.* This alleged missing link was discovered by Eugene Dubois's expedition in 1891 along the Solo River in Java (now Indonesia). The fossil evidence for Java Man indicated to some scientists that it lived 500,000 years ago. However, a closer look at the initial dating process and skull cap and femur bones suggest that it is either a human or ape but not both.
- *Lucy.* In 1974 while in Ethiopia, Donald Johanson discovered the remains of an animal that allegedly lived more than 3 million years ago. It is still debated whether Lucy is a small human or a chimpanzee.
- *Ramapithecus.* In 1932 several teeth and jawbones were found in India. These were thought to belong to an early ape-man dating from about 14 million years ago. However, anthropologists have since discovered that they belong to an ape.

- *Neanderthal Man.* Neanderthal Man was thought to be the remains of an early ape-man. But recent studies have provided convincing evidence that he was a hunched man who suffered from a vitamin D deficiency.[17]

Is creation a science?

According to evolutionists, creation—the belief that God supernaturally created the world apart from any evolutionary processes—should not be taught as "science." We are told that creation is a matter of *faith* and evolution is a matter of scientific *fact*, and that creation should be taught in church but never in the science classroom. Critics say that the idea of a "Creator" is religious and not scientific and, therefore, should be excluded from the public classroom. For Christians, however, this couldn't be farther from the truth. The evolutionists' understanding of creation is both misdirected and mistaken for many reasons.

First, creation is scientific. Evolutionists fail to see the difference between "operation science" and "origin science." How things *originate* can be wholly different from how things *operate*. Both macroevolution and creation are theories of the origin and development of life that are classified under *origin* science, the study of past events that only occurred once. *Operation* science, on the other hand, observes the *present* workings and operations occurring over and over again in our universe. Since evolution and creation are not occurring today, neither can be studied directly using operation science.

To put it simply, origin science seeks to understand what happened in the past; whereas, operation science attempts to understand the present observable workings of things. Origin science addresses past *singularities,* and operation science observes present *regularities*. Origin science looks at how things *began*, and operation science focuses on how things presently *operate*.

Origin scientists accomplish their investigation by piecing together clues that were left behind. In contrast, operation scientists conduct firsthand observations and repeated testing. Origin science approaches evolution and creation by viewing and reconstructing the evidence that remains (because creation and evolution can't be repeated in the laboratory today). This occurs when scientists discover bones, animal, or plant remains (fossils). These remains can tell scientists about what happened in the beginning, when life first emerged. This way of studying theories of origins is done much the same way police scientists (forensic experts) gather evidence after a homicide occurs. Because police didn't observe the actual crime, these experts must gather clues to piece together what probably happened in the past. The study of evolution and creation is approached the same way. Just because creation isn't approached using *operation science* doesn't mean that it can't be studied using the methods of *forensic* or *origin science*. The following chart will help clarify the differences between origin and operation sciences.[18]

Origin Science	Operation Science
Studies the past	Studies the present
Studies *singular* events	Studies *regular* events
Studies unrepeatable events	Studies repeatable events
Concerned with how things began	Concerned with how things continually work
Creation/evolution	Astronomy
Discovers *what* happened in the *past*	Discovers *how* something happens in the *present*

Evolutionists often make the mistake of confusing the role and limitations of the two sciences. To do so would be equivalent to measuring air temperature with a wind velocity instrument; it's a category mistake.

Second, just because creation is found in a religious book (the Bible) doesn't mean that it's not scientific. Other well-known sciences study objects that are found in the Bible. For example, geologists study rocks, archaeologists dig for artifacts, paleontologists examine the remains of living things, and biologists investigate the origins and operations of living creatures. Does this mean that geology, archaeology, paleontology, and biology are not scientific? Of course not! If evolutionists reject creation as science because it is found in a religious source, we must also reject the other major sciences.

Third, it is obviously wrong to reject something simply because of its source. To reject something because of its source is called a "genetic fallacy" in logic. This fallacy is seen in Nathaniel's statement concerning Jesus, when he asked, "Can anything good come out of Nazareth?" (John 1:46). Source does not determine truth!

If the same people who reject evidence because of its source applied the same restrictions consistently, they would have to restrict the teachings and influence of the popular philosopher Socrates. This is because his call to philosophy was given by a Greek prophetess, a *religious* source. Further, most government institutions would have to forbid the use of overhead projectors because the idea for an alternating-current motor came in a vision Nikolai Tesla had while reading a pantheistic poet.[19] Society would come to a grinding stop if this logic were applied consistently to everyone.

Fourth, if the facts that support creation are not taught because they are associated with religion, facts that support evolution also should be excluded because they favor the religious position of secular humanism. Yes, atheism is a religious position! Several atheistic religions exist, such as Taoism, some forms of Buddhism, and secular humanism. For example, the father of modern education, John Dewey, was a "religious humanist." Dewey and others felt so strongly about religious humanism that they agreed to formulate their own doctrinal statement in 1933 called the *Humanist Manifesto.* Their most obvious claim is that they consider humanism to be a *religion* even though they *deny* the existence of God. In the statement they make their beliefs evident.

> To establish such a religion is a major necessity of the present. It is a responsibility which rests upon this generation. We therefore affirm the following:
> *First:* Religious humanists regard the universe as self-existing and not created.
> *Second*: Humanism believes that man is a part of nature and that he has emerged as the result of a continuous process.
> *Third:* Holding an organic view of life, humanists find that the traditional dualism of mind and body must be rejected . . . .
> *Sixth:* We are convinced that the time has passed for theism, deism, modernism, and the several varieties of "new thought."[20] (Interestingly, these humanistic beliefs are opposite of our Declaration of Independence.)

Forty years later (1973) the humanists drafted a second manifesto that made even clearer their disbelief in the existence of God and their support of the theory of evolution. It reads: "As in 1933, humanists still believe that traditional theism, especially faith in a prayer-hearing God . . . is an unproved and outmoded faith. . . . Science affirms that the human species is an emergence from natural evolutionary forces."[21]

As seen above, evolutionary curriculum agrees perfectly with the secular humanist religion that denies the existence of God. If evolutionists are consistent with their view of limiting the teachings of creation because of its association with Christianity and the Bible, they should also limit their own teaching since evolution is a central belief of the secular humanist religion.[22]

Fifth, the facts that support creation can be studied without it being "religious." Creation can be examined in a public setting without worshiping God or believing the Bible is true. We can approach the facts of creation from a *detached, objective, and academic* point of view much the same way a geologist studies rocks without being religious. Even though rocks are religious objects of worship to some people, this doesn't make the geology professor "religious." The choice to worship the Creator, or a rock for that matter, is entirely up to the individual.

Further, all schools have rules of behavior that prohibit cheating, rape, or even theft. Even though these rules of conduct are totally compatible with the Bible, it would be incorrect to say that the school is "religious" and, therefore, must eliminate these moral rules.

To take the evolutionists' way of thinking to the extreme, we would have to call our leaders in government "religious leaders" because they often give us laws that are compatible with religious beliefs. Several of the Ten Commandments found in Exodus 20 have been adopted as law in our country. For instance, our law prohibits murder, false witness under oath, and stealing. Just because something is compatible with a religion doesn't make it religious.

If creation curriculum is excluded from the classroom simply because of its association with Christianity, then so should the rest of the sciences because of their association with religion. After all, science examines objects that are worshiped or used in religious rituals, such as rocks, trees, animals, stars, bones, the sun, and the forces of nature.[23]

Sixth, many overlook the fact that modern natural science was largely influenced by early European scientists who believed in a supernatural creation of the universe. They did have a desire to study nature as God's creation because of what they might learn about God and His established order in the world. Among those who laid the foundational principles for which modern science is indebted are:[24]

- Johannes Kepler (1571–1630): celestial mechanics, physical astronomy
- Blaise Pascal (1623–62): hydrostatics
- Robert Boyle (1627–91): chemistry and gas dynamics
- Nicolaus Steno (1638–87): stratigraphy
- Isaac Newton (1642–1727): calculus and dynamics
- Michael Faraday (1791–1867): magnetic theory
- Louis Agassiz (1807–73): glacial geology and ichthyology
- James Young Simpson (1811–70): gynecology
- Gregor Mendel (1822–84): genetics
- Louis Pasteur (1822–95): bacteriology
- William Thomson (Lord Kelvin) (1824–1907): energetics and thermodynamics
- Joseph Lister (1827–1912): antiseptic surgery
- James Clerk Maxwell (1831–79): electrodynamics and statistical thermodynamics
- William Ramsay (1852–1916): isotopic chemistry

Why do many scientists accept evolution as fact?

If evolution is untrue, why do so many teachers and students believe it's a fact? Many textbooks and magazine articles portray evolution as an undisputed champion of the origins and development of life. They show countless pictures of the latest "new" bone discoveries and emphatically declare that our great ancestors were apelike creatures. Some professors, who have vigorously supported evolution, make those who doubt or question evolution's credibility feel like ignorant outcasts. There are at least three reasons why many secular academicians accept it as fact.

1. Some scientists overestimate the evidence for evolution. In an evolutionist's zeal to discover clues that prove evolution's credibility, he tends to overlook problems with the evidence itself. The ape-man discoveries discussed earlier serve as ample evidence of initial excitement that only evaporates months later after the truth is discovered. Unfortunately, by the time the truth about the newfound evidence

is known to the public—if they hear it at all—the media has already published the findings as fact.

2. Some teachers present evolution as fact and the students blindly accept it. Most students go through school never questioning the evidence. The story of life is usually one-sided and rarely appeals to any significant representation of creation. Consequently, this lopsided view is then carried into life without ever being sufficiently investigated or critically examined. As a result, when conversation about evolution or creation arise, it is easier for the student to favor the position he is most familiar with—evolution.

3. Some people believe evolution is fact because they have absorbed it by "osmosis." Television and radio shows incorporate different components of evolution into scripts. This is accomplished most subtly in many cases. After watching television or listening to radio for several years, these evolutionary components become more familiar and are quickly accepted as true. Why? Because the script presents evolution as an indisputable fact that every "reasonable" person should believe. To question evolution would be equal to questioning your own existence! Before you know it, you are well indoctrinated in evolutionary philosophy without enrolling in a single college class.

Conclusion

In the end, evolutionists must answer three crucial questions:

1. How does something come from nothing?
2. How does life come from nonlife?
3. How does intelligence come from nonintelligence?

There is little doubt as to the impact of the theory of evolution upon the world. It has been broadly accepted by secular colleges and universities. We know, however, that truth is established evidence not majority vote. The evidence for creation far outweighs the scant evidence for evolution. Fortunately, scientists now have access to more information and technology than Charles Darwin ever dreamed. Ironically, scientist Robert Jastrow accurately assesses the scientific pursuit: "For the scientist who has lived by his faith in the power of reason, the story ends like a bad dream. He has scaled the mountains of ignorance; he is about to conquer the highest peak; as he pulls himself over the final rock, he is greeted by a band of theologians who have been sitting there for centuries."[25]

Review

1. List the two basic components that define the theory of evolution. _____

_____

_____

_____

_____

_____

2. Describe the difference between "chemical evolution" and "biological evolution." _____

_____

_____

_____

_____

_____

3. Describe the difference between "microevolution" and "macroevolution." _____

_____

_____

_____

_____

_____

4. List at least three problems with the theory of macroevolution.

(1)_____

_____

_____

(2)_____

_____

_____

(3)_____

_____

_____

5. How does the fossil record support creation?

_____

_____

_____

_____

_____

6. Why couldn't a simple living cell have originated by slow evolutionary processes? _____

_____

_____

_____

_____

7. What is "natural selection"? _____

_____

_____

_____

_____

_____

CHAPTER 6
What about Other Worldviews?

Scenario

In the school cafeteria for lunch, Jennifer and Sarah find each other.

Jennifer: At least this time we didn't collide. If we had, we might have started a food fight. You know, after our biology class, I got kinda sick to my stomach looking at the fish and chips over there. It made me feel like I was going to eat a distant relative or something!

Sarah: Eeeew! Now you've got me thinking about this hamburger. We'll just have to evolve into veggie heads!

Jennifer: See, creation at least makes our food look and taste better!

Sarah: OK, but if I agree with you about creation, can you guarantee me an *A* on our biology exam on evolution?

Jennifer: No, but if you'll put your trust in Jesus, I can promise that you'll get the ultimate and eternal *A*.

Sarah: How did I know that was coming? Like I'm not knocking you or putting you down or anything. Your religion is fine for you, but it just doesn't work for me. There are too many religions and holy men like Jesus to chose from. So, you know, different strokes for different folks, right?

69

Jennifer: Yes, there are a lot of religions, but they all can't be true,
           especially because their beliefs are so different.
Sarah: How do you know which one is true?
Jennifer: Well . . .

Questions

- How should Jennifer respond?
- Are all ideas about religions essentially the same?
- How is the Christian worldview different?

Purpose

To become familiar with the vital role worldviews play in how
people understand reality

Goal

To understand how to defend Christianity against worldviews
that challenge it

In this chapter you will learn

- that a worldview is the *interpretive framework* or *lens* through
  which we understand our world.
- that the seven alternative worldviews are in direct conflict
  with the Christian worldview (theism).
- that a good worldview is logical, consistent, practical, and
  comprehensive.
- that the Christian worldview best explains our world as it exists.

What is a worldview?

Now that we know God caused the universe, let's define and
evaluate other perspectives about Him. These perspectives are called
"worldviews." Worldviews are simply how we view the world in
which we live. In other words, worldviews are the glasses, lenses,
grid, or framework through which we interpret or understand what
we see, hear, and otherwise experience. For example, if we wear sun-
glasses that have yellow lenses, we will see everything that occurs in
the world as yellow.

Today, about six billion people live on our planet, and all of us
use our own set of glasses (worldviews) to make sense of God, the
world, values, truth, and historical events. This is why people come

to different conclusions about God even when viewing the same set of facts. People may agree on the facts themselves, but they come to various conclusions about what the facts mean.

You see, facts don't come with instruction manuals on how to interpret them. Viewing the facts through our worldviews produces our interpretation. For example, atheists who view the facts surrounding Jesus' resurrection will come to different conclusions than Christians. Atheists may interpret the facts and conclude that the Resurrection was an unexplainable phenomenon that had no scientific basis or explanation. The notion that God doesn't exist—which eliminates all acts of God as possible explanations—largely influences the atheistic conclusion. They may even offer an explanation that appeals to purely natural means.

On the other hand, Christians will interpret the fact of the Resurrection quite differently, namely, as a miracle of God. To put it simply, miracles are impossible in the atheists' worldview but possible in the Christians' worldview. The importance of a worldview is that it makes a world of difference in how we interpret facts.

What do other worldviews believe?

Seven major worldviews exist, and six of them are in direct conflict with Christianity. Each view has its own defining characteristics that are embraced by various movements and religions.

Theism

This worldview believes God exists as the infinite personal Creator of the world beyond and in the universe. Christians have adopted this worldview. It is important to remember that theism is unlike atheism in that theism maintains that God can act supernaturally in the natural world. Three major religions represent theism: Judaism, Islam, and Christianity.

Deism

Persons who embrace deism believe God exists as the infinite personal Creator of the world beyond the universe but is not active in it. Deism is like theism but without miracles. God created the universe but remains distant from it. He does not involve Himself in a direct way. This view believes God simply wound up the universe like a clock and allows it to run on its own.

Finite Godism

This worldview claims that a finite God exists in and beyond the universe but is limited in power. Finite godism embraces a God who can create the world but doesn't have the power to sustain it or assure victory over evil. This perspective portrays a struggling Creator engaged in constant battle with His creation to overcome moral rebellion. Although no religion currently adopts this view, occasionally some Christians' view of God is no greater than a finite god.

Atheism

Atheism is the belief that God does not exist anywhere in the universe or beyond it. This worldview denies God's existence altogether. Unlike theism, which affirms God's existence independent of human beings, atheism completely rejects the idea and believes man invented the reality of God. Within an atheistic world, evil is real; however, no devil or ultimate moral standard exists by which to live. Morality either depends on the situation or is completely relative. Atheism views the universe as "all there is"—there is nothing beyond it—and atheists believe the universe arose purely by chance, without any intelligent cause whatsoever.

Pantheism

God *is* the universe for persons who embrace pantheism. This worldview asserts that God is identical with the universe; there is no distinction between the Creator and the created. Pantheists believe God is all, and all is God, including people. Because pantheists believe people have forgotten or are ignorant of their real divine nature, they are encouraged to "remember" or "realize" it through meditation—oftentimes, to achieve the goal of "enlightenment." According to many pantheists, logical thinking can make one falsely believe there are distinctions instead of believing that all is one divine reality. Pantheism, with its emphasis upon the presence (immanence) of an ultimate reality, is recognized as the polar opposite of deism, which stresses God's distance (transcendence). Certain forms of Buddhism, Hinduism, Christian Science, and the New Age movement have adopted pantheism.

Panentheism

This worldview asserts that God is *in* the universe. Although it sounds much like pantheism, there are many differences. Unlike pantheists, who believe that God *is* all, panentheists assert that God is *in* all. They believe that God is in the world much like a soul is in the body or a mind is in the brain. In other words, God has two aspects of existence: finite and infinite. The finite world is God's body, and the infinite side is the immaterial aspect located beyond the world. Since the world changes, God changes also.

Polytheism

Polytheism claims that many finite Gods exist beyond and in the universe. This worldview is the only perspective that is compatible with pantheism. For example, Hinduism believes in an infinite impersonal One (Brahman), which manifests itself in personal forms known by the names of individual gods. In the ancient world, the Romans, Egyptians, and Greeks believed in polytheism. In modern times, Mormons, Hindus, and witches also cherish polytheism. Unlike deists' distant and detached God, the gods the polytheists believe in are active in the world to bring about either healing or harm. Polytheism takes many forms. Some gods are said to have been birthed by the forces of nature (sun, wind, sea, etc.), and others possess characteristics of virtue (love, truth, light, compassion, etc.). Each god is believed to have its own sphere of influence. In Hinduism, millions of gods are responsible for certain events, such as war, creation, and preservation.

Which worldview is right?

As Christians, we should strive to help others discover the correct worldview. In chapter 4 we showed reasons why Christians believe in theism, let's focus now on evaluating the strengths and weaknesses of each view. When evaluating, remember that a good worldview must possess several components:

1. It must be *logical* and *consistent* with the facts already known to be true. If a worldview is contradictory or incoherent, avoid it (1 Timothy 6:20). After all, who wants to live by something irrational or in conflict with itself? This means that it cannot have any self-defeating premises such as "we know we cannot know anything."

Worldviews in Conflict

Worldview	Theism	Deism	Finite-Godism	Atheism	Pantheism	Panentheism	Polytheism
View of God	One infinite God	One infinite God	One finite God	No God	One infinite God	One God with finite and infinite poles	Many finite Gods
Religion or Philosophy	Christianity Judaism Islam	Some forms of liberalism	Plato John S. Mill Rabbi Kushner	Secular-humanism; Marxism; Buddhism*	Hinduism Buddhism* New Age	None/A. N. Whitehead	Mormons Witchcraft Early Greeks
Relationship of God to the world	Beyond and in the world	Beyond the world	Beyond the world and struggling in it	Only world exists	God *is* world	God is *in* the world	Many gods active in the world
Personality of God	Personal	Personal	Personal	None	Impersonal*	Personal	Personal
Miracles	Yes	No	No	No	No	No	Yes
Nature of Truth and Values	Absolute	Absolute	Relative	Relative	Relative	Relative	Relative
Afterlife	Resurrection of soul/body	Soul-rewards or punishment	Soul-rewards or punishment	Cease to exist	Reincarnation	Remembered by God	Gods reward or punish
Jesus	Unique God/man	Only man	Only man	Only man	Guru or manifestation of God	Only man	One of many gods
Man's Problem	Sin/rebellion against God	Sin/rebellion against God	Ignorant/Imperfect	Lack of education	Ignorance of the divine self	Illusion/Ignorance	Man fails to appease the gods

*Often or some

2. If a worldview is true, it must be *practical* and *livable*. A worldview that doesn't offer application or an interpretive framework through which we can understand reality on a day-to-day basis is useless. We expect a truthful worldview to be useable; however, we must not think all livable worldviews are true. Atheists may say they have a livable and productive outlook on life and reality, but this doesn't make their worldview correct. The test of practicality and livability alone can't tell us which worldview is true, but it can give us a good idea of which is false.

3. A good worldview must be *all-encompassing* and *comprehensive*. It doesn't ignore the tough questions of life, such as the nature of God, evil, morality, or the world in which we live. Christians believe theism is the one worldview that can best explain the world as it exists today while at the same time being consistent with the truths of both science and the Bible.

Using the above three characteristics as a judge, the following evaluation will explain why Christians reject all other worldviews and accept theism as the best option.

Theism

For several centuries theism has been criticized as being outdated for modern people. It has also been tabbed a by-product of humankind's wishful thinking. However, four solid reasons support the claim that theism is true.

First, theism offers a "first cause" to the origin of the universe that is consistent with the scientific principle of causality: "Everything that has a beginning needs a cause."

Second, theism possesses an absolute unchanging basis by which we can make moral decisions. Because this value standard exists above, beyond, and in the world, it can serve as ultimate judge and jury for conflicts between individuals, cultures, and the world's moral systems.

Third, theism offers meaning and hope to millions of people worldwide. Its concept of rewards and punishments is a powerful motivating factor that encourages moral living. Personal deeds within a theistic worldview count not only for time but also for eternity. Those who have experienced suffering have found hope and comfort within a theistic worldview because of its emphasis on the afterlife (Revelation 21:4).

Fourth, the God of theism is perfect in every way; therefore, He is worthy of our ultimate worship. Unlike the worldviews that have a less-than-perfect god, theism maintains that ultimate worship should only be given to an ultimate being. All too often, adherents of other worldviews render ultimate devotion to one who is less than ultimate.

Deism

Deism has largely been dropped as a valid worldview even though some liberal churches have preserved deist beliefs. Deism has made some positive contributions to the variety of worldviews, but three weaknesses center on miracles and God's relationship to people.

1. The deist belief that God miraculously created the world is inconsistent with their disbelief in miracles. If God accomplished the biggest miracle of all (Creation), why then can't He achieve lesser miracles like the resurrection of the dead?

2. Deists seem to ignore the evidence that supports the miracles of the Bible. The abundant eyewitness testimony to the miraculous events recorded in Scripture give us good reason to conclude they are real. If deists reject these testimonies, they also must reject our entire judicial system, which relies on eyewitnesses as the principle means of establishing the truth of a matter.

3. The belief that God is distant from the universe and not active in it has led many to believe God is detached and impersonal. A God who is not active in the world can't possibly identify or be concerned with the pressing needs of His creation. It's reasonable to assume that if God miraculously created the world for the good of His creatures, then from time to time He would miraculously act in their lives for their own good. Why would God abandon His creatures if He could help them? Alternatively, if God had decided to condemn His creation because of humankind's sins, why hasn't He destroyed it? If God will not or could not help His creatures, then we must question whether He is all-powerful and all-loving.

Finite Godism

Finite godism has correctly pointed out that the Christian God is limited by His very nature. This means there are some things God can't do. For example, God can't lie (Hebrews 6:18), tolerate evil (Habbakuk 1:13), deny Himself (2 Timothy 2:13), or embrace contradictions (1 Timothy 6:20). However, a finite god is less than adequate for several reasons.

First, a finite God needs a cause of His existence. Remember, finite beings have a beginning. The law of causality states: "Everything that has a beginning needs a cause." If a god needs a cause, He is not really God. Only an infinite God without a beginning doesn't need a cause.

Second, a finite God isn't worthy of ultimate worship and devotion. To worship a finite being is to commit idolatry. It is to give ultimate worth to something that isn't ultimate.

Third, many finite godists don't believe in an infinite, all-powerful God because evil still continues in our world without any apparent cure. This belief can be quickly overcome, however, by pointing out that because evil is not destroyed *now* doesn't mean it won't be destroyed in the *future.*

Atheism

Atheism has been a healthy correcting influence to theists who wish to sharpen their skills. Many of the reasons atheists use to defend their view of the world have forced Christians to refine and revise their own arguments to make them stronger. Unlike pantheism, atheism has acknowledged the reality of evil and injustice in the world. However, three fatal flaws in atheism need to be addressed.

1. Atheists do not have a first cause of the universe. In the past, many atheists believed the universe was eternal. This belief has largely been abandoned since science has discovered that the universe had a beginning (i.e., the big bang theory). Within atheism, no first cause exists. Many of them say that swirling gases, dust, and atoms were the cause. However, we would have to ask, what or who caused the gases, dust, and atoms? In other words, the atheist's view doesn't answer the question of origins.

2. Natural forces do not explain the origin of the universe. Why? Because the cause that brought the universe (nature) into existence must be beyond nature (that is, super-natural). If atheists recognize that the presidential faces on Mount Rushmore needed an intelligent cause, why then do they fail to see that the intelligent design present in the universe (DNA molecules and anthropic principle) implies a designer's existence?

3. Atheists do not have an ultimate moral standard by which to call the world evil or unjust. The atheist would not know evil or injustice unless he had an ultimate standard of good and justice by which to evaluate it. For instance, nobody can call a line crooked unless he first has a straight line by which to compare it.

Pantheism

Although pantheism has several problems that make it unacceptable to Christians, it should be commended as a worldview that attempts to explain all of reality. Pantheists have rightly pointed out that a *distant* God (deism) cannot relate to people. Nevertheless, four important characteristics of pantheism fail the test for truth.

1. Pantheists can't explain how people have come to forget their own divine nature. What happened in the distant past to account for this universal spiritual amnesia?

2. Pantheism is logically inconsistent with its own claims about God. On the one hand, God is unchanging; on the other hand, some pantheists desire to be enlightened through meditation, which calls for change in consciousness. If people are God, they can't change because the unchangeable can't change (Malachi 3:6).

3. Pantheism fails to be a livable worldview. If all is God, what happens when you cut the grass? Are you cutting God? Critics of pantheism often point out that when a pantheist is in the path of an oncoming car, he quickly jumps out of the way. Is God getting out of the way of Himself? There would be no reason for Him to protect Himself if He is identical to the car.

Further, to believe that all is one and God is identical to the world poses another problem: no distinctions can be made. Yet the pantheist distinguishes his worldview from another and walks *around* material objects instead of *through* them. Failure to make distinctions between pantheism and theism, good and evil, sin and righteousness, male and female, and Christ and Satan makes it impossible to distinguish truth from error. Yet pantheists believe their view is true and opposing views are false.

4. Setting aside logical thinking has its problems. Most pantheists assume that logic does not apply to God; however, it has been pointed out that pantheists actually use logic to eliminate logic. For example, the statement "logic doesn't apply to God" self-destructs

because the very statement applies logic to God. In short, pantheists believe it is logical to set aside logic to gain enlightenment.

Finally, an impersonal God can't possibly be concerned with or relate to the suffering of people. Pantheists may try to avoid this problem by denying suffering and people really exist. This is unacceptable for two reasons. First, it is impossible to prove anyone's nonexistence. Why? Because a person would have to exist in order to affirm he or she doesn't exist. Second, to say evil doesn't exist is not comforting to those who are experiencing it. If their suffering is an illusion, why are they having these kinds of illusions? Why do they seem so real?

Panentheism

Panentheism is often confused with pantheism; however, there are several differences. Unlike most forms of pantheism, panentheists affirm the existence of a *personal* God who relates to the world. While pantheists believe God is impersonal and identical to the world, panentheists believe God is *in* the world just as a soul is in the body or a mind is in the brain. That is to say, God has two poles: physical (the world) and spiritual—one infinite and the other finite.

Contrary to pantheism, panentheists should be recognized for preserving the individuality of God, the world, and humanity. Nevertheless, there are at least two crucial problems with panentheism.

1. The panentheist's concept of an infinite-finite God is actually impossible. Many have pointed out that an infinite-finite is a contradiction in terms. This is because an infinite being is not dependent upon anything for its existence, yet a finite being is dependent on another and therefore needs a cause of its existence. To believe God is both infinite and finite at the same time is like believing a drinking glass is full of water and not full at the same time and in the same sense.

2. A finite God can't guarantee final victory over evil. The God of panentheism is a struggling God who must learn and grow toward perfection as history unfolds. If God learns from the evil that humans have experienced in the past, then He is using us as pawns on the chessboard of life to better His own nature.

Polytheism

Polytheism is the belief that many finite gods exist. Despite this unsubstantiated position, it has had a positive effect. How? Polytheism's emphasis on the existence of a spiritual realm and the need for humankind to discover the gods has brought an awareness to many unbelievers that we are not alone in the universe. Nonetheless, polytheism has three crucial problems.

1. If forces of nature birthed the gods, why not worship nature as divine? Unlike theism, polytheism attributes superiority to nature as the cause of the gods. This makes nature ultimate and not the gods; thus, nature becomes a substitute for God.

2. Human minds invented the gods of polytheism. To better understand human characteristics and how the forces of nature work, people became superstitious and began applying virtues (love, hate, compassion, etc.) and natural names (sea, wind, etc.) to the gods. As a result, any natural disaster such as a hurricane, flood, or earthquake was quickly thought to be divine punishment. These calamities further prompted the people to begin appeasing the gods by satisfying their requirements.

3. The polytheists' belief that the world is eternal is contrary to scientific facts. The first verse in the Book of Genesis declares, "In the beginning God created the heavens and the earth." Science has supported this beginning by discovering the expanding universe from a point of beginning and the second law of thermodynamics, which says the universe is running down. (See "First-Cause Proof" in chap. 4 for an explanation of the expanding universe and the second law of thermodynamics.) If the world is eternal, the scientific data should reflect evidence compatible with this theory, which is not the case.

Conclusion

Within the maze of worldviews, we have discovered that only theism offers a logical, consistent, and livable view of the world. All other views have crucial problems that disqualify them for thinking Christians. Knowledge of the various worldviews will greatly enhance your apologetic and evangelizing efforts as you accurately apply Scripture and reason to the flaws inherent to other worldviews.

Review

1. What is a worldview? _____

_____

_____

_____

_____

_____

2. List and define each of the seven worldviews.

(1)_____

_____

_____

_____

(2)_____

_____

_____

_____

(3)_____

_____

_____

_____

(4)_____

_____

_____

_____

(5)_____

_____

_____

_____

(6)_____

_____

_____

_____

(7)_____

_____

_____

3. Describe the difference between pantheism and panentheism.

_____

_____

_____

_____

_____

_____

4. How has your worldview influenced the way you act toward others? _____

_____

_____

_____

_____

_____

5. What are the three tests used to evaluate worldviews?

(1)_____

_____

_____

(2)_____

_____

_____

(3)_____

_____

_____

6. Give at least three reasons why theism is the best worldview.

(1)_____

_____

(2)_____

_____

(3)_____

_____

7. Which religions ascribe to theism, pantheism, and atheism?

_____

_____

_____

_____

_____

_____

CHAPTER 7

If God Exists, Why Evil?

Scenario

As Peter and Jordan find their seats in their first class of the school day, the principal addresses all the students over the public address system.

Principal: May I have your attention please? A few minutes ago two jet airliners were deliberately crashed into the two World Trade Center towers in New York City. The local news reported that there were probably thousands that have been killed. If any of you have family that could be affected by this tragedy, please report to the office as soon as possible. Thank you.

As class dismisses, Peter and Jordan are shocked.

Jordan: Can you believe it? How could someone just crash those planes into innocent people?

Peter: That's horrible! I hope not many people got hurt.

Jordan: The principal said the news reported several thousand may have died. . . . Peter, what are you doing?

Peter: I'm praying. Lord, please help those people. I know you care about them.

Jordan: If the Lord cared about them, why did he allow this to happen? It doesn't make sense. How can God be all-good,

loving, and powerful and yet these evil things still occur?
These things should never happen in the first place, right?

Peter: Good question. Uhhh . . .

Questions

- How is Peter going to explain that the absolutely good God can coexist with evil?
- If God has the power to stop evil, why doesn't He?
- Why do we suffer if God loves us?

Purpose

To provide an answer to the alleged contradiction between the all-loving and powerful God and the existence of pain, suffering, and evil

Goal

To make sense out of the existence of God in light of the presence of evil in the world

In this chapter you will learn

- that evil originated as a result of Lucifer exercising his free will against God's will.
- that we are responsible for our own choices.
- that evil is real but not a real thing or object.
- that God allows evil to remain in the world because He has a purpose for it.

One of the most common objections to Christianity, and perhaps the greatest barrier to faith in Christ, is the presence of evil in light of God's existence. How can the loving God allow evil into the world? After all, the Bible says everything God has made is "good" (Genesis 1:31), that nothing is unclean of itself (Romans 14:14), every creature of God is good (1 Timothy 4:4), and to the pure all things are pure (Titus 1:15).

Nevertheless, evil is here! Just ask anyone who has been a victim of violent crime or who has endured pain and suffering. Indeed, evil is a reality. In this section, by answering several questions, we will attempt to explain the presence of evil in view of the existence of the all-good and powerful God.

Where did evil come from?

How then could evil ever emerge from the perfectly good creation created by the perfectly good God? It may seem impossible. Many people automatically blame God for the evil in the world, when, in fact, its origin wasn't directly from God—it was from humans and angels (Satan; Isaiah 14:12; 1 Timothy 3:6; Jude 6–7).

But how could perfectly good people like Adam and Eve, who didn't have sin natures originally, bring evil into the world? The answer is remarkably simple: by their *own free choice*. Let's look at this answer more closely.

God created Adam and Eve with the perfection of free choice, which is the ability to choose one thing or another without being forced to choose either one. Adam and Eve used their free choice when they decided to disobey God and eat from the forbidden tree in the garden of Eden. At that point, evil emerged on earth, and it came as a by-product of human decisions—free acts of disobedience. Yes, evil came from something good: free will.

To help you understand how evil may come from something good, take, for instance, the blacksmith who shapes a red-hot horseshoe on his anvil. As he hammers to form the smoldering horseshoe, a spark flies off his hammer and sets the barn in which he is working on fire. Ultimately, the barn is completely destroyed. The good blacksmith shaping a good horseshoe with good fire burned down the good barn. Just as the burned-out barn was a by-product of something good, such as horseshoe making, evil also is the result or by-product of something good, such as free choice.

At this point, many of you may be wondering, *Why?* If God knew that free choice would give rise to evil, why did He give us free choice? He did so because the ability to choose is quite important. It is the very ingredient that makes our love of God and of each other meaningful (Matthew 23:37).

What if we were all robots preprogrammed to say "I love you"? This love would be about as meaningful as a pull-string doll that repeats the phrase "I love you, I love you, I love you." There would be no personal decision to love; and without that decision, there could be no salvation because salvation depends on our decision to love and receive Christ (Romans 10:9–10). To summarize it all, the ability to love by freely using our choice is more important than God eliminating all evil at this time, and He would have to abolish free choice to eliminate evil. To be clear, God created the fact of freedom and man creates the acts of freedom. God made evil possible, but man makes evil actual.

Who is responsible for Adam and Eve's sin?

Some suppose that either God or Satan was responsible for Adam and Eve's sin because neither of them had a sin nature before they ate of the forbidden tree. Although the Bible records Satan tempting Adam and Eve (Genesis 3), several reasons reveal that it is wrong to blame Satan.

First, Satan's effort was a *contributing* cause of the sin but not a *determining* cause. Yes, Satan influenced, contributed, and used persuasion to get Adam and Eve to make a decision of disobedience. Nonetheless, Adam and Eve chose to disobey by exercising their own free will. This is made clear when we realize that all actions, whether obedient or disobedient, need a cause. Actions don't just happen without any rhyme or reason, cause, or actor behind them. The fundamental law of causality, which was discussed while offering proofs for God's existence (see chap. 4), applies to human acts as well. The same law of causality that was used to demonstrate God's *being* (i.e., existence) can also be used to demonstrate humankind's *doing* (i.e., actions). Adam and Eve's actions to disobey God were either

- uncaused . . . This option violates the law of causality, which says every event (actions are events) needs a cause. It is impossible for an event to arise without a cause.
- caused by another . . . If Adam and Eve's sin had been caused by Satan or another influence, God couldn't have held them responsible for their actions. They could have said, "The devil made us do it!" But it is clear that God found them guilty and pronounced judgment (Genesis 3:13–19). Further, if our actions are caused by someone or something else, how could the judicial system ever convict criminals for the evil actions (crimes) they commit? A criminal could simply say, "The devil made me do it." In other words, the consequences of believing that our acts are caused by another would eliminate individual moral responsibility.

- or caused by myself . . . This option seems to be the only reasonable solution to account for the original sin. Adam and Eve's actions were caused (determined) by their *self* (i.e., I, me, self). Self-caused actions preserve the individual's moral responsibility and account for a first cause of the action (sin) itself.*

The second reason we can't say that Satan was the determining cause of Adam and Eve's sin is because if we did we would still have to answer the question who tempted Satan to sin? The truth of the matter is, no other being persuaded or encouraged Satan to sin. *There was no tempter before Satan fell.* God did not tempt Satan or influence him in any way because James 1:13 says, "Let no one say when he is tempted, 'I am tempted by God'; for God cannot be tempted by evil, nor does He Himself tempt anyone." Satan, who had no sin nature originally, sinned of his own free decision to disobey God.

Therefore we come to the following conclusion: if God, in whom there is no darkness at all (1 John 1:5), couldn't have made Adam and Eve sin, and their decision to disobey God wasn't caused by another (Satan), *then Adam and Eve were responsible for their own sinful actions.*

What is evil?

When trying to define evil, the major world religions have had different responses. Some say evil doesn't really exist. Others say it is a contagious virus. Still others believe it is a material object with molecules as solid as a rock or a piece of furniture.

The Christian view of evil, however, is much different. Christians believe evil is real but not necessarily a real *thing*. Yet, if God created everything and evil is something, does this mean God created evil? No! Although this answer may seem to be a contradiction to some, if we look closer, it is evident that evil is something different.

Evil can be easily understood when we remember that it is something real but not something *material*. If evil were material, we could

---

* To avoid confusion with chapter 4 (p. 44), it is important to remember that even though we say our actions can be "caused by ourselves" and the universe must be "caused by another," we mean that both the universe and our actions need first causes. In the case of the universe, the first cause is God; in the case of our actions, the first cause is our self. The difference between *self* and *actions* is that self "decides" what course of action to take and the actions themselves follow from the decision as a *result*. We do not mean that actions are the first cause of themselves. *Also see* Norman Geisler, *Chosen but Free* (Minneapolis: Bethany House Publishers, 1999), 24–27.

charge God with evil since He made the material world of rocks, trees, minerals, and oceans (Genesis 1:1). Such a charge, however, is inconsistent with what we already know to be true about God, namely, that everything He made was "good" (Genesis 1:27–31). Besides, the apostle John said that "no darkness at all" is in God (1 John 1:5). This means that evil has to be immaterial.

Evil is actually a lack in something good. For example, holes in the side of a car caused by rust or an accident could be considered an evil because the car would be lacking or missing the element that should be present—metal. In a spiritual sense, the lack of a proper relationship to God was the main evil that resulted when Adam and Eve decided to disobey Him and eat the forbidden fruit.

To take explaining evil a bit further, here's a tricky question: Is the lack of an eyeball on a rock considered evil? No, because the rock shouldn't have an eyeball in the first place. Remember, evil is a lack of something that *should be present* in the first place. Therefore, the absence of sight in a stone is not evil, but the lack of sight in a person is an evil though nonmoral in kind.

Evil also can be understood in terms of bad relationships.[1] For example, picture an archer's good hand pointing a good arrow on a good bow at a good person. Shooting the arrow at the person would result in a bad relationship. The material things involved are not evil in themselves (Romans 14:14), but the resulting relationship between the things is lacking. Similar examples are guns or tornadoes ripping through a populated area. The things involved are not evil in themselves; only if there exists a bad relationship between other things can it be considered evil.

Why doesn't God stop all evil?

The presence of evil throughout the world seems inconsistent of an all-powerful God to allow it to continue. It would appear that if God were all-powerful, then He could eliminate evil. If He were all-good, then He would destroy evil. But the truth of the matter is that evil is not destroyed. Many people therefore conclude that there cannot be a perfect God. This attitude leaves many Christians in a quandary. How do we explain the existence of evil in light of an all-powerful and all-good God? The Bible says Jesus conquered evil, nailing "it to the cross" (Colossians 2:14–15) and that the reason for His coming was to "destroy the works of the devil" (1 John 3:8);

however, a quick reading of a local newspaper reveals the fact that evil actions are becoming more common. Is there a contradiction here? No. Although God *is* all-powerful and all-good, there are at least four reasons why He will not stop all evil at this time.

1. Jesus' work on the cross did indeed defeat evil. In what way? He defeated evil *officially* in His first coming and will overcome evil *actually* in His second coming. This means that when Jesus died on the cross and rose from the dead, He removed the guilt and penalty of our sin in order to make a new relationship possible between us and God. In other words, we now have a new official position in Christ free from the evil consequences—eternal punishment (2 Corinthians 5:21). When Christ returns a second time, however, He will *actually* separate Christians from the evil we now see around us (Matthew 25:31–46; Revelation 21:4). At that time He will provide a place for evil, called "hell," and a place for good, called "heaven" (Matthew 25:31–46). In short, Jesus defeated evil the first time with the *cross*, but next time He will defeat it with the *crown*. God made the defeat of evil *possible* at His first coming but will make its defeat *actual* at His second coming.[2]

2. For God to stop evil completely now, He must first *eliminate all free choice*. Yes, freedom of choice must be stopped before evil can be totally abolished. This is because evil is a by-product of free decisions. As we have seen, if God eliminated free choice entirely, then we could never make a choice to receive Jesus as Savior, and there would be no heavenly fellowship with God. Freedom is the very thing we have that makes it possible to *meaningfully* love God. Jesus said that love is the greatest commandment (Matthew 22:36–37; 5:22–48). If we were forced to love God without the ability to freely choose, we would be no better than lifeless robots. Furthermore, it would be inconsistent with God's eternal purpose and will that all should have the opportunity to freely participate in His eternal fellowship (2 Peter 3:9).

3. To believe that God doesn't exist because evil is not yet defeated is unreasonable. Just because evil is not currently destroyed doesn't mean that God will not defeat it in the future. If the nonbeliever applies this same way of thinking to scientific issues, he will be proven wrong. For example, scientists previously did not know what caused earthquakes, tornadoes, or even bumblebee flight. Today they have the answers to these puzzling questions. Likewise, even though

evil is not *yet* actually defeated, in the future we will see the final act of God's plan to abolish evil altogether and more fully understand why He waited.

4. To say that God doesn't exist because evil is still present is simply unreasonable because no finite being knows for sure what the future holds. Just because God is all-powerful and all-good doesn't mean He must destroy evil *now*. Rather, if God is all-powerful, He *can* destroy evil; and if He is all-good, He *will* destroy evil. Our finite minds simply do not know *when*.

Is there a purpose for evil?

When evil strikes, it is hard for most of us to understand why it happened. Why did a friend loose her arm in a car accident? Why did Mom die of cancer? Why did my house burn down? WHY? WHY? WHY? Few of us can see any good purpose in tragic events that cause pain and suffering. These tough "why" questions are usually met with attempts to comfort—such as hugs or consoling words—that often fall short of an adequate answer that will lessen the pain.

The nonbeliever would say that because an all-good God must have a good purpose for everything, and because there seems to be no good purpose in pain and suffering, it is therefore logical to deny the existence of an all-good God. Actually, there are many reasons to reject this kind of thinking and remain strong in our faith even when evil strikes and leaves us confused about God's purpose and existence.

First, we know there are some good purposes for evil. God often makes us aware of greater evils that could arise by using lesser evils as warning signs. For example, the pain of a toothache warns us of a cavity. If not taken care of, it could require a root canal or other dental surgery (ouch!). Pain is often necessary to keep us from destroying ourselves. The first time we were burnt with a hot kitchen pan or an automobile engine was not fun, but it made us aware of the need to avoid hot materials. If we didn't learn, there could be even more severe consequences that could result in the form of losing life or limb.

Second, we may not know every purpose God has for evil, but that doesn't mean there is none. It is unreasonable to assume that God has no good reason for evil just because we are unaware of it. In fact, the apostle Paul said, "How unsearchable are His judgments and His ways past finding out! *'For who has known the mind of the LORD?'"* (Romans 11:33–34).

Third, God allows evil in order to ultimately defeat evil. Jesus' death on the cross is a good example. Jesus suffered whippings, beatings, and cursings as an innocent man. God permitted this evil—the pain, suffering, and death of Jesus—in order to ultimately defeat evil in the long run (John 15:13; Hebrews 12:2). God had a higher purpose in removing forever the penalty of sin by allowing evil to occur in the process of Jesus' death. God permitted an evil *injustice* (Christ's death) to occur to *one person* (Jesus) in order to accomplish *mercy* for the *many* (humankind).

God has good purposes for the evil that we may encounter even though we don't understand it. For example, Joseph was betrayed through an evil plot by his brothers to sell him to a caravan of Ishmaelite traders on their way to Egypt. When Joseph was later reunited with his brothers in Egypt due to a severe famine, he said to them, "But as for you, you meant evil against me; but God meant it for good, in order to bring it about as it is this day, to save many people alive" (Genesis 50:20).

Could God have avoided evil?

Couldn't God have created a world in which no evil existed? Some say God shouldn't have created the world in the first place because He knew some people would be evil and go to hell. Nevertheless, God did create a world with free creatures in which evil is present. Why did He choose this way of accomplishing His purposes rather than another? Let's look at several reasons why God may have thought the present way was the best one.

First, God could have created a world where no evil existed (He did when He created Adam), but He could not guarantee it would stay that way as long as *free* creatures live in it. If God had forced Adam (or the rest of us) to always choose good, then Adam wouldn't have been free. Forced freedom is a contradiction. If it's forced, then it's not free, and if it's free, it's not forced. As said before, evil is a *by-product* or possible consequence of freedom. God would have to sacrifice freedom in order to keep evil away, and this He will not do because free choice is necessary to receive all moral good, including salvation. When all free decisions to accept or reject Christ have been made, evil will be separated from us forever (Revelation 21–22). Stated succinctly, "This present world is not the best of all possible worlds, but is the best way to get to the best possible world with free creatures involved in the process."[3]

Second, to say that for us to avoid evil and hell, God shouldn't have created anything, is to say nothing is better than something. Try applying that same logic to your favorite sporting event. Should we stop playing the Super Bowl because we know that one team will eventually lose? How about Wimbledon tennis? Should we abolish this popular championship because we know one player will be defeated? Of course not! Having the opportunity to succeed, risk, and win is a greater good than not having that chance at all. The same reasoning applies to why God created the world: even though God knew there would be some losers, the opportunity to love, live, and receive Jesus as Savior is better than not having any chance or opportunity whatsoever. That is, something is better than nothing.

Finally, God chose this way to accomplish His purposes because it is the most *reasonable* way to complete His plan of triumphing over evil and rewarding good. God can protect free choice and ultimately win over evil by using a process of "separation"—those who choose against Christ will be separated from those who choose to receive Christ. Those who are separated from God in the afterlife will never corrupt good again, and those who receive heaven by their faith in Christ will not sin or disturb believers anymore. Yes, God will defeat and separate evil according to our free choice! In other words, good and evil will eventually be totally separated and confined, never to infringe on each other again (Revelation 20:11–21:8). This process will give birth to a reality in which evil is overcome and a perfect world exists.

Of course, there are those who say God can't achieve a perfect world while sending people to hell because sending people to hell shows that God isn't perfect. There are at least three reasons why this way of thinking is unfounded.

1. God doesn't send anyone to hell; He simply *confirms a person's free decision* to live apart from Christ. Although God wills that all should be saved (2 Peter 3:9), He would be unloving if He *forced* people into heaven against their will. Forced love is a contradiction in terms. God will not do this. Just as we can't force people to love us, neither will God force us to fellowship with Him if we have first declined His invitation to do so. If God's will is for all people to be

saved, and some have been lost, does this prove that God's will has been thwarted? No, because God wills some things unconditionally such as His own existence and other things conditionally such as man's salvation. This means there are no conditions under which God can ever go out of existence or tell lies to us because He is irreversibly bound by His own nature (look up Malachi 3:6; Hebrews 6:18). On the other hand, salvation is will by God under one condition—your choice to receive Christ (Romans 10:9–10).

2. God is not unfair because people are in hell. He would be unfair only if there were someone in hell who shouldn't be there.

3. God can achieve and enjoy a perfect world knowing that some are in hell just as I can enjoy a meal although you have declined to eat. Moreover, we must also remember that God is perfect in all He does, whether it is heaven or hell. What does not come under his *perfect grace* (salvation and heaven) returns under His *perfect and righteous judgment* (hell).

Conclusion

Although the scars of evil have had their devastating effects upon humanity, the Christian can look forward to inheriting a perfect world where evil is separated and isolated forever. No more crying, pain, suffering, or any kind of evil will touch our blissful existence with Christ (Revelation 21:4). The process God is using to accomplish His plan with free people is not only sensible, it is the only way to bring about a perfect world.

Review

1. How did evil originate? _____
_____
_____
_____
_____
_____

2. What is evil? _____
_____
_____
_____
_____
_____

3. Describe how evil can be understood in terms of "bad relationships." _____

_____

_____

_____

_____

_____

_____

_____

4. Why doesn't God stop evil now? _____

_____

_____

_____

_____

_____

5. List some good purposes for evil. _____

_____

_____

_____

_____

_____

6. What precious gift would have to be destroyed if God were to abolish evil right now? _____

_____

_____

_____

_____

_____

CHAPTER 8

Are Miracles Possible?

Scenario

As the last bell dismisses the students for the day, Peter, Jordan, Sarah, and Jennifer hurry to Peter's house to check the latest news of the tragedy on television. As they turn on the television, Sarah begins to cry.

Jennifer: Are you OK, Sarah?

Sarah: Yes, I'm just really worried about all those people around the two buildings who may have been killed.

Jennifer: Me too. Let's pray. Lord, please comfort those families who have lost loved ones in the buildings. Give them hope that they will one day see them again after the resurrection. Thank You, Jesus, for rising from the dead and paving the way for others to follow. Amen.

Jordan: How can someone rise from the dead? It's impossible.

Peter: It's possible with God because He is all-powerful and sent Jesus to prove it.

Sarah: Do you guys really believe in miracles and all that stuff? It sounds far-fetched.

Peter and Jennifer: Uhhh . . .

Questions

- What is a miracle?
- Have you ever witnessed a miracle?
- Do you believe that miracles are possible?
- How do miracles support the gospel message of salvation?

Purpose

To establish the evidential value and purpose of miracles as they relate to the Christian faith

Goal

To understand both the importance and necessity of defending the existence of miracles

In this chapter you will learn

- that there are good reasons to accept the possibility and believability of miracles.
- that a miracle is a rare and purposeful event caused by God in the natural world that could not otherwise have occurred on its own. It is an act of God that suspends the laws of nature.
- to defend the possibility of miracles because Christianity is based on the miraculous event of the resurrection of Jesus. If there are no miracles, then there was no resurrection and no Christianity!
- that authentic miracles are always instantaneous, successful, and specific; people never relapse to a former condition, and they occur in a moral and theological context.
- that miracles are possible in light of the laws of nature because these laws don't *dictate* how the universe *must* operate, rather they *describe* how the universe *usually* functions.
- that biblical miracles are believable because we have reliable eyewitnesses and historical records.

Now that we know God exists and that the real existence of evil is not inconsistent with an all-good God, let's turn our attention to the subject of *miracles*. The Bible is filled with miraculous events, from Genesis to Revelation. Jesus walks on water, heals the sick, turns water into wine, casts out demons, multiplies loaves and fishes for the hungry, and raises the dead. Moses parts the Red Sea, Peter raises the dead, and Paul withstands a viper attack. Yet all of these events are viewed as "impossibilities" by modern scientific experts.

How can Christians rationally explain such events in a world that rejects the supernatural? In the natural world, people sink when trying to walk on water, and they usually fail when attempting to raise the dead. The radical, miraculous claims in Scripture seem to be in direct conflict with our everyday experience. This in turn has set up a stumbling block for many who find Christianity to be unbelievable. It is not the purpose of this chapter to prove that all miracles listed in Scripture have actually taken place; that is a historical question answered by the eyewitnesses (see chap. 9). Our goal in this section is to show that miracles are both *possible* and *believable*.

What is a miracle?

To guard against confusion when speaking about miracles, it is important to define them. By the word *miracle,* we mean a divine intervention into the natural world. It is a supernatural exception to the regular course of the world that would not have occurred otherwise.[1] This definition reveals several characteristics of miracles.

First, miracles are special acts of God that produce a purposeful event. Because miracles are acts of God, we know that the source or origin of miracles is not from the natural world in which we live. Instead, they have a supernatural cause. That is to say, miracles occur *in* the world, but they are not *of* the world.

Second, the "purpose" associated with miracles helps us distinguish them from random, unusual events. For example, let's say you and a friend are walking on the beach. As you begin to share Christ, he brings up objections. In an effort to make your presentation more credible, you tell your friend that God will make a whale leap out of the ocean and fly for ten minutes. As you begin to pray, a whale suddenly leaps out of the sea and begins to fly. Would this be considered a miracle? Yes! It had *purpose and timing,* and it *fit the situation.* Could this same event be identified as a miracle if you hadn't been witnessing or praying for such an event in the first place? No, because the *purpose* and *timing* of the *situation* would have changed. This would be considered an "unusual" event, but we could not know it was miraculous without these identifying characteristics.

Why defend miracles?

Miracles are important for at least four reasons.

1. Christians need to defend miracles because our faith is supported by the most important miracle of all—the resurrection of Jesus. If miracles are not possible, then the Resurrection never happened. Without this special event, the apostle Paul tells of the dark consequences that follow (see 1 Corinthians 15:12–19), namely, Christianity would be false.

2. Miracles serve as God-given signs directed at us to confirm His message of salvation, power over death, and His ability to fulfill His promise to resurrect all Christians. After all, Jesus made extraordinary claims about Himself and the afterlife that are hard for some people to believe. This being the case, God gave us accompanying proofs (miracles) that confirm that what He says is indeed true (see Hebrews 2:2–6). In this sense, miracles are God's evidence to unbelievers. This is precisely what places Christianity above the rest of the world's religions. Other religious systems don't possess true confirming miracles as Christianity does. Without these miracles, the words of Christ would be like empty promises without any reason to believe He has the power to fulfill them.

3. Miracles bring glory to God. This is achieved by confirming His Word (Hebrews 2:3–4), the messenger (Acts 2:22), and the message (Exodus 4:1–9; 2 Corinthians 12:12). His power and awesome character is displayed wherever miracles occur. They should draw us deeper into worship and adoration of His Holy Being whenever we see His power unleashed.

4. Miracles are sometimes used to confirm that an inward reality, such as the forgiveness of sin, has actually taken place. In other words, anyone could say "Your sins are forgiven," but how does someone really know if they truly are forgiven? Since forgiveness can't be observed with the naked eye, God has attached a miracle that can be observed as proof of forgiveness. For instance, when the Pharisees confronted Jesus about His authority to forgive sins, Jesus responded, "But *that you may know* that the Son of Man has power on earth to forgive sins . . . I say to you, arise, take up your bed, and go to your house" (Mark 2:10–11, emphasis added). Since the Pharisees couldn't tell whether the man was actually forgiven, Jesus gave them evidence by miraculously healing the man. God

does not ask us to believe what He says blindly, but rather provides us with the evidence we need in order to make an informed decision. The Christian faith is not a wild leap in the dark; it is a step of faith in the light of the evidence.

How can you tell the difference between miracles and magic?

Many of us know about or have observed the extraordinary feats of magicians like David Copperfield, Houdini, or even the bizarre exploits of an Eastern guru. For many people these magical works seem to be on the same level as biblical miracles. However, there are certain important characteristics that clearly differentiate the two.[2]

First, biblical miracles are always instantaneous, never gradual. If Jesus healed someone, it was immediate and complete. This is much different from our modern-day "prophets" who declare to some that miraculous healing comes gradually. (There is one two-stage miracle in the Bible: the blind man in the Gospel of Mark [8:22–25]. However, each stage was immediate and complete.)[3]

Second, biblical miracles are always successful. A true miracle has never failed. This is because God is the source and originator of the act, and man is the instrument that God uses.

Third, there never is a relapse after a genuine miracle. This means that if Jesus heals a disease, that disease never comes back again. Of course, those who were raised from the dead died again (Matthew 27:52–53; compare Romans 5:12), only to await their permanent resurrection (1 Corinthians 15:12f).

Finally, all miracles are specific, not vague or obscure. Jesus' miracles were of pinpoint accuracy, leaving no doubt as to the nature of the miracle He desired to accomplish. Whether the problem was demonic, physical, or spiritual, Jesus identified it *specifically* to avoid any confusion about His objective.

The following columns make a clear distinction between miracles and magic by comparing their different characteristics.[4]

Miracles	Magic
Are under God's control	Is under man's control
Are done at God's will	Is done at man's will
Are not repeatable	Is naturally repeatable
Have no deception involved	Has deception involved
Occur in nature	Does not occur in nature

Fit into nature	Does not fit into nature
Are unusual but are not odd	Is unusual but also odd
Are associated with good	Is often associated with evil
Bring glory to God	Bring glory to man
Used to confirm God's Word	Used to entertain or deceive people

Are miracles possible?

The importance of miracles can't be ignored by any serious Christian because the very existence of Christianity as a believable religion is at stake. Namely, if miracles are not possible, then there is no Christianity. Christ's resurrection, deity, virgin birth, and second coming would all be considered myths, much like "Snow White and the Seven Dwarfs."

Even though there have been many objections to the possibility of miracles, there is one obvious criticism that we must address. *How can a miracle occur in our world where the laws of nature are considered unbreakable?* To gain a better understanding of these laws, let's look at a few.[5]

The "laws of nature" include such conditions as gravity, earth rotation, occurrence of night and day, tidal changes, and season changes, all of which are observed by scientists to occur on a *continuum* and reflect a *never-ending cycle* of nature. Many say that these laws can't be violated, stopped, or suspended for any length of time. However, we know this to be false by simply observing a plane at the airport overcome the law of gravity as it departs for its destination. Our goal as Christians is to show that these "laws" are not fixed and unbreakable and that *miracles can break into our world whenever God desires.* We can achieve this in several ways.

First, we need to show that miracles do not have to obey these natural laws the way we must obey traffic laws. The two are totally different *kinds* of laws. The main difference is that traffic laws tell us how we *should* operate, and natural laws tell us how the world *usually* operates. In other words, traffic laws are not expected to be violated because they tell us what we *ought* to do. However, there can be exceptions *to* natural laws by the occurrence of miracles because natural laws only describe what customarily occurs in the natural world. In this sense, a miracle is not really a "violation of"; it is an "exception to" or "suspension of" the laws of nature. This "exception to" can be likened to the canceling of the daily scheduled school routine for a special assembly. A miracle is simply an exception to the normal routine of nature. After the miracle has been accomplished, the laws of nature continue on their regular course in the world.

Second, if God exists (chap. 4), then acts of God (miracles) are possible. This is just as reasonable as saying, "If humans exist, then acts of humans are possible." Besides, God's will supersedes the laws of nature. Indeed, it is His will that created and sustains these laws (Hebrews 1:2–3). In the final conclusion, the only way to prove the impossibility of miracles would be to prove that God doesn't exist. Indeed, because the evidences show that God created the universe, the biggest miracle has already happened (see chap. 4).

Are miracles believable?

There are some who agree that miracles are conceivably *possible*, yet they still have problems saying they are *believable* or *plausible*. Usually this doubt in miracles is due to the absence of personally experiencing them. The doubter would argue that since miracles *rarely* occur, we shouldn't believe in them. When was the last time you experienced a resurrection or someone walking on water? Most of us haven't. Therefore, according to the doubter, this shows that the evidence against miracles is greater than the evidence for them. However, there are two flaws with this line of thinking.

1. Just because most of our life experience is absent of biblical miracles doesn't mean they shouldn't be believed. If we are to disbelieve miracles because we don't experience them, we must also disbelieve that the Revolutionary War ever took place because we didn't experience it either. What about the great San Francisco earthquake in 1906? How about the very beginning of life or any other event that occurred only once in the past as did miracles? None of these events are being experienced today. Should we doubt their existence? No, because we have reliable eyewitness reports that were written down to inform future generations. Likewise, we have written eyewitness accounts to inform future generations of the believability of miracles that have occurred in the past.

2. Those who disbelieve miracles because our experience against them is greater than our experience with them, make the mistake of *adding* the evidence instead of *weighing* the evidence.[6] Adding up the number of days in our lifetime on which we never experience miracles

and comparing it to the number of days that we do experience miracles is not treating the evidence fairly. "Weighing" evidence is much different than "adding" evidence. To weigh evidence means to evaluate its quality and measure its trustworthiness in order to come to a conclusion. Adding is simply looking at the quantity of evidence from the day a miracle didn't occur rather than weighing the evidence on a day when one did occur.

Our United States judicial system places greater value on only *one* eyewitness testimony over *ten* testimonies of people who never saw a given crime. What testimony do you think would be more valuable to the court when deciding what to believe: the one witness who saw the crime or the ten people who didn't? So it is with miracles. Even one reliable eyewitness would be enough evidence to believe the miracles contained in the Bible. We should base our beliefs on what people *do* see and experience, not on what they *don't* experience. Just as the ten people who never witnessed the crime should have no direct bearing on the court's decision (they could have only an indirect or circumstantial value as such and may have none at all), so, also, the many people who have never experienced miracles should have no bearing on whether to believe miracles or not.[7]

Conclusion

Miracles play an important part in God's plan to reach a lost and searching world. They provide us with evidence to support what Jesus said about Himself, and they bring glory to God. Without these special acts of God, we would be left without any confirming proof that Christianity is true. The kind of evidence God has left us far exceeds that of any other religion in quality. Indeed, miracles are what separate Christianity from the host of other religions.

Review

1. What is the definition of *miracle?* _____

_____

_____

_____

2. List several characteristics of miracles._____

_____

_____

_____

_____

_____

_____

3. Why must Christians defend the possibility of miracles?

_____

_____

_____

_____

_____

4. How do miracles differ from magic? _____

_____

_____

_____

_____

5. What purposes do miracles serve? _____

_____

_____

_____

_____

6. How do miracles bring glory to God?_____

_____

_____

_____

_____

7. Why should we believe miracles are possible?

_____

_____

_____

_____

_____

CHAPTER 9

Can the New Testament Be Trusted?

Scenario

The next day at school, Peter, Jennifer, Jordan, and Sarah are eating lunch together as they discuss Christianity.

Sarah: These hamburgers are great!

Jennifer: Yeah, I'm getting stuffed. Thank God for burgers.

Jordan: Speaking of God, how do we really know what He's like? I mean, everyone writes books about Him and has their own opinion. Where do you find the truth?

Jennifer: The Bible.

Peter: Yeah, the Bible tells us all about God and Jesus— especially the New Testament because it records what Jesus did and said.

Sarah: But how do you know the New Testament hasn't been corrupted or changed over the years? Can you trust it? After all, man wrote it.

Peter: Uhhh . . .

Questions

- Does the New Testament offer an accurate account of what actually happened?
- How do you know or find out whether someone is telling the truth about an event?
- Do you think the New Testament is historically reliable?

Purpose

To establish the New Testament as historically reliable by presenting various supporting evidence

Goal

To understand the crucial role the New Testament plays in providing us with historically, scientifically, and spiritually reliable information regarding the deity of Christ (see chap. 10) and the inspiration of Scripture (see chap. 12).

In this chapter we will learn

- that historical and scientific statements about people, places and events in the New Testament are as important as spiritual statements about forgiveness and the afterlife.
- that we have good reason to believe that the New Testament we have today is a trustworthy copy of what the original New Testament said.
- that there are many crucial pieces of evidence such as manuscripts, archaeology, history, prophecy, and science available to demonstrate the reliability of the New Testament.
- that the alleged conflict between the Bible and science is not due to facts, but rather to the conflicting interpretations of fallible scientists and fallible theologians.

The previous chapters have shown that (1) apologetics is necessary, (2) there is truth that can be known about God, (3) there are good reasons to believe He exists, (4) God has purposes for evil, and (5) miracles are real. Most of our study has not used Scripture for support in case someone didn't believe the Bible was true. These previous chapters would strengthen our reasoning skills as a supportive tool to reinforce and clarify scriptural principles.

Let's now turn our attention to the first topic in our third and final step (evidential apologetics) in the apologetic goal: the reliability of the New Testament. We want to know if Scripture can be trusted in what it says about itself, Jesus, and historical events, such as the Resurrection. Once the New Testament's reliability is established, we can look at what it says about the deity of Christ (see chap. 10) and the inspiration of Scripture. This is necessary because

without a reliable New Testament, there is no trustworthy information on the divine nature of Jesus and the inspired character of the
New Testament.

Why is it important?

It is no surprise to many of us that there are some who don't
believe the New Testament is the Word of God. Thus the importance of defending its trustworthiness can't be ignored. If the New
Testament is in error on anything—whether that error is historical, scientific, spiritual, or even mathematical—then God's error-
less character has been demoted to the human level. The logic is
clear: if God can't err, and the Bible is the Word of God, then the
Bible can't be in error. If someone fails to believe that the New
Testament is telling the truth about *earthly* matters such as history
and science, how is he going to believe the *heavenly* message of forgiveness of sin?

If the New Testament is wrong in earthly matters that can be
easily verified (such as historical events), then it would be unreasonable for someone to believe Scripture when it talks of unseen spiritual things (such as forgiveness, the afterlife, and angels) that can't be
verified as easily. Jesus made this point very plain when He spoke to
Nicodemus and said, "If I have told you earthly things and you do
not believe, how will you believe if I tell you heavenly things?" (John
3:12). If we can't trust the New Testament in the simple things, how
will we trust it in the more complicated? Similarly, without a reliable
New Testament, there is no historical way to know who Jesus is or
what He said or did.

Can't the Bible defend itself?

Not all Christians feel it is necessary to show evidence for the New
Testament because they believe that if it is the Word of God, then it
will stand and speak for itself. After all, the Word of God is "living and
powerful" (Hebrews 4:12). Granted, if the Bible is the Word of God,
it will speak for itself; but how do we know the Bible we possess today
is an accurate representation of the original Word of God written
two thousand years ago? The Mormons, Muslims, Buddhists, Hindus,
and others say that their Scriptures speak for themselves. How do we
discover which book should be trusted? We must look at the *evidence* to
discover whether we ought to believe the New Testament.

All of us had some reason why we believed the New Testament to be telling us the truth, as opposed to believing some other religious book or fairy tale. It could have been because the message of Scripture simply agreed with common sense and possessed power never before experienced in life. Maybe the historical events of Scripture were confirmed to you in history books. Could it have been the shining reflection of Jesus within the person who witnessed to you? Whatever the reason for believing, one thing is clear: God commands us to use reason (Isaiah 1:18; Matthew 22:37) to tell the difference between truth and error (1 John 4:6) and right from wrong (Hebrews 5:14).

How can we trust the New Testament when it's two thousand years old?

The writers of the New Testament began their work in the first century, only twenty to thirty years after the death and resurrection of Jesus. Wow! That's a long time ago. Usually writing materials fade and disintegrate after a few hundred years. What makes the New Testament so special? Its lasting message has survived the test of time, and there are several reasons for this.

First, God's Holy Spirit has supernaturally overseen the Bible from the beginning to ensure that later generations will have it to read. In other words, it is *indestructible* (Matthew 5:17–18) and *unbreakable* (John 10:35).

Second, the Bible has survived throughout the centuries because it has been copied and recopied. The men who copied it were called "scribes." They would take the Bible and copy every word over a period of several months with the utmost care and reverence. The copies that were made are called "manuscripts." Manuscripts are important not only because they preserve Scripture for later generations, but because Bible scholars and students can collect hundreds and thousands of them to compare and discover how accurate they are. For example, if one manuscript that was copied in Egypt was missing a verse, a Bible scholar could compare it with manuscripts copied in Israel in order to find the missing verse. The more manuscripts you have to compare, the better.

Let's apply this idea to something all of us know about—textbooks. What if your apologetic study guide was missing a page? To discover what the page said, you would get another manual to fill in the information that was missing. It is the same process with the New Testament. Since we don't have the original writings, scholars compare manuscripts in order to piece together what the original copy said.

The New Testament alone has more than 5,600 Greek manuscripts. Greek was the original language in which the New Testament was written. There are more than fifteen thousand more manuscripts in other various languages. These manuscripts are evidence that shows us that our New Testament is essentially the same message that was written down two thousand years ago.

No other piece of ancient literature can boast this many manuscripts. The conclusion is clear. If unbelievers can't trust the New Testament because they can't be sure that it represents the original writings, they must also reject all of ancient history, science, philosophy, and poetry due to the inferior manuscript evidence.

Can we trust the New Testament if we don't have the original writings?

The answer is *yes!* We can trust the New Testament because we have *good copies.* We don't need the originals to be able to preserve the message of Scripture. In the New Testament as we have it today, we do have the Word of God and the complete, vital truth of the originals. For example, would you question the trustworthiness of the Declaration of Independence or the United States Constitution if it were destroyed or lost? Of course not. Why? Because we have copies that represent what the original said. The same is true for Scripture; there is no reason to doubt what the original writers passed to us because we have thousands of copies.

Is the New Testament telling the truth about history?

Many people today believe the New Testament tells us the truth when speaking of spiritual matters such as sin, salvation, and the afterlife. However, it is not limited to spiritual truths. It goes far beyond them into the historical and scientific areas. Yes, the Bible is true when touching on spiritual, historical, and scientific statements. This is a very important point. After all, if the writers of the New Testament didn't tell us the truth about people, places, and events, how can we trust what they say about spiritual matters (John 3:12)? When we question the historical accuracy of the Bible, we are also seeking to discover whether the New Testament we possess today is a trustworthy source about Jesus. In other words, did Jesus actually do and say all that is written of Him? For several reasons we believe the New Testament is historically accurate.

First, as stated before, the New Testament contains reports of eyewitnesses to the works and words of Jesus. These people were alongside Jesus; they actually saw Him and heard Him (Luke 1:1–4; John 19:35; 21:24; 2 Peter 1:16; 1 John 1:1–4). In today's society, eyewitnesses are important because they help the courts discover who is telling the truth. Our United States court system values eyewitness testimony. Consequently, if someone rejects the eyewitness accounts of the New Testament, he must also reject the role of eyewitnesses in our judicial system.

Second, non-Christian Roman historians support the trustworthiness of Scripture through their written records. One such historian named Tacitus, who lived through the reigns of at least six Roman emperors (A.D. 56–120) is best known for his two books *Histories* and *Annals.* Within these books he references events that occurred in the Gospels (Matthew, Mark, Luke, and John). The following list of New Testament events show a remarkable agreement with non-Christian historical references.[1]

1. Christians were named after their founder, "Christ" (Christians; see Acts 11:26; 26:28).

2. Jesus had been executed in Tiberius's reign (see Luke 3:1) by the governor of Judea, Pontius Pilate (see Luke 23:24–25).

3. The gospel message was taken to Rome (see Acts 28:16).

4. Christians were persecuted and nailed to crosses (see John 15:20).

5. Some Christians were persecuted and killed by wild animals (see Hebrews 11).

The non-Christian Roman historian Seutonius (born A.D. 70) refers both to Jesus and to Christians in his writings. Seutonius is best known for *Twelve Caesars,* in which he writes of the events surrounding the reigns of twelve Roman emperors, from Julius Caesar to Domitian. He makes the following two references:[2]

1. The Emperor Claudius told the Jews at Rome to leave the city because they were blamed for certain disturbances, which were instigated by Christ (see Acts 18:2).

2. Christians were being persecuted and tortured by Emperor Nero (see Acts 26:28).

Then there was Josephus, a Jewish historian who worked for the Roman government. His historical writings also indicate that the New Testament is trustworthy. For example, Josephus names James as Jesus' brother (see Matthew 13:55; Acts 15:13) and Pontius Pilate as the one who condemned Jesus to the cross (see Luke 23:24–25). He also speaks of the ministry of John the Baptist (see John 1) and to Jesus Himself.

All the above examples from non-Christian historians should open our eyes to the trustworthy character of the Bible. Notice what historian A. N. Sherwin-White, who specializes in Roman history, says about the history of the Book of Acts: "For Acts the confirmation of historicity is overwhelming . . . any attempt to reject its basic historicity even in matters of detail must now appear absurd. Roman historians have long taken it for granted."[3]

Third, the early dates attributed to the Gospel of Luke and the Book of Acts give us good reason to believe that the writer was a reliable eyewitness or contemporary of the reported events. Roman historian Colin J. Hemer provides the following crucial evidence that Acts was written between A.D. 60 and 62:[4]

1. There is no mention in Acts of the crucial fall of Jerusalem in A.D. 70.

2. There is no mention of the outbreak of the Jewish war in A.D. 66 or the deteriorating relations between the Romans and Jews.

3. There is no hint of the deterioration of Christian relations with Rome during the Neronian persecutions in the late 60s.

4. There is no mention of the death of James at the hands of the Sanhedrin in c. 62.

5. The prominence and authority of the Sadducees in Acts reflect a pre-70 date, before the collapse of their political cooperation with Rome.

6. Luke gives details of the culture of an early Julio-Claudian period (Acts 18:2).

7. Areas of controversy described presume that the temple was still standing.

8. The confident tone of Acts makes it unlikely to have been written during the Neronian persecution of Christians and the Jewish war with Rome during the late 60s.

Further, Hemer lists numerous specific details of places, names, conditions, customs, and circumstances that support the historical nature of Luke's eyewitness account of the events recorded in Acts.[5] Many have been confirmed by historical and archaeological research, including the following:

1. A natural crossing between correctly named ports (Acts 13:4–5)

2. The proper river port, Perga, for a ship crossing from Cyprus (13:13)

3. The proper location of Lycaonia (14:6)

4. The unusual but correct declension of the name *Lystra,* the correct language spoken in Lystra, and the correct name of the two gods associated with the city, Zeus and Hermes (14:12)

5. The proper port, Attalia, for returning travelers (14:25)

6. The correct route from the Cilician Gates (16:1)

7. The proper form of the name *Troas* (16:8)

8. A conspicuous sailors' landmark at Samothrace (16:11)

9. The proper identification of Philippi as a Roman colony and the right location of the river Gangites near Philippi (16:13)

10. The association of Thyatira with cloth dyeing (16:14) and the correct designation of the titles for the colony magistrates (16:20, 35–36, 38)

11. The proper locations (Amphipolis and Apollonia) where travelers would spend successive nights on their journey (17:1)

12. The presence of a synagogue in Thessalonica (17:1) and the proper title of *Politarch* for the magistrates (17:6)

13. The correct explanation that sea travel is the most convenient way to reach Athens in summer due to favoring east winds (17:14)

14. The well-attested cult of Artemis of the Ephesians (19:24, 27) and that the Ephesian theater was the city meeting place (19:29)

15. The correct identification of Ananias as high priest (23:2) and Felix as governor (23:34)

16. Agreement with Josephus of the name *Porcius Festus* (24:27)

17. Correct identification of the best shipping lanes of that time period (27:4)

18. Correct description of the severe liability on guards who permitted a prisoner to escape (27:42)

19. Accurate description of the local people and superstitions (28:4–6)

20. Common practice of custody with a Roman soldier (28:16) and conditions of imprisonment at one's own expense (28:30–31)

The overwhelming confirmation of these details gives evidence that Acts is historical. No other ancient book has this amount of detailed confirmation. What's more, not only is it confirmation of Acts; it is also an indirect confirmation of the other Gospels since Luke also wrote his Gospel before A.D. 60, and it parallels both Matthew and Mark.

Fourth, the science of archaeology provides further evidence that the New Testament is reliable in matters of history. Archaeologists seek to uncover lost and buried remains of ancient civilizations so they can gain an understanding of their history and culture. These remains can be buildings, pottery, coins, stone inscriptions, tools, or even weapons. All of these findings can be used to show the trustworthiness of Scripture. The following are a few examples of archaeological evidence that supports the Bible:

1. The pavement mentioned in John 19:13 was recently discovered in the court of the Tower of Antonia (which is a military fortress).

2. The "Pool of Bethesda" mentioned in John 5:2 had no record of existence except in the New Testament. However, in 1888 some of it was found while digging near the Church of Saint Anne.

3. The time period of the governor Quirinius mentioned in Luke 2:2 has been confirmed by discoveries unearthed by archaeologist Sir William Ramsey. He found writings that tell of Quirinius being governor of Syria on two different occasions.

4. The mention of "Pilate" who tried Jesus

In light of these discoveries, note what archaeologists have said about the Bible:

- Nelson Glueck states, "It may be stated categorically that no archaeological discovery has ever contraverted a biblical reference. Scores of archaeological findings have been made which confirm in clear outline or exact detail historical statements in the Bible."[6]
- Millar Burrows asserts, "More than one archaeologist has found his respect for the Bible increased by the experience of excavation in Palestine."[7]
- Sir William Ramsey says, "Luke is a historian of the first rank; not merely are his statements of fact trustworthy . . . this author should be placed along with the very greatest of historians."[8]
- William F. Albright records, "Aside from a few diehards among older scholars, there is scarcely a single biblical historian who has not been impressed by the rapid accumulation of data supporting the substantial historicity of the patriarchal tradition."[9]

History is of the utmost importance to Christian doctrine. Why? Because Jesus often made historical statements that served as a *sign* or *foundation* for Christian doctrine. For example, when Jesus was approached by miracle seekers in Matthew 12:39–40, He responded by saying, "No sign will be given to it except the sign of the prophet Jonah. For as Jonah was three days and three nights in the belly of the great fish , so will the Son of Man be three days and three nights in the heart of the earth." Jesus made a historical statement by referring to the events of Jonah as He used it as a sign of His own resurrection that was to come. Notice the connection between *history* and Christian *doctrine* of the resurrection. Unless the historical event of Jonah was true, how could it possibly be a sign to nonbelievers of Jesus' resurrection?

The fact of the matter is clear—without history there is no Christianity. For instance, without the historical events of Jesus' death on the cross and His resurrection, there is no forgiveness of sin. Without the historical virgin birth, there is no Jesus who preached in Palestine two thousand years ago. History, along with Christianity's unique belief system, is the very ingredient that separates historic Christianity from mythology and fables. Unlike other religions, Christianity is dependent on the historical reliability of critical events and miracles.

Is the Bible scientifically true?

Yes! First of all, as just noted, the Bible has been confirmed by the science of archaeology. Further, the Bible made amazingly accurate scientific statements about our universe almost three thousand years before modern science discovered these scientific truths. Even though the Bible is not a scientific textbook you would use in your biology class, one of the great wonders of the Bible is its scientific respectability. Although some disagree and claim the Scriptures are "unscientific," the Christian position views the Bible as simply "prescientific." For this reason, there are many who see the Bible and science as two very different enemies seeking to destroy each other.

Actually, the Bible and science are closely related. We must remember that God created both the entire natural world—the universe (Genesis 1:1), which is the domain of science—and the truths of the Bible (2 Timothy 3:16). The Bible and nature can't be separated because they are both revelations from God. Why then is there so much disagreement between science and the Bible? When answering this question, it is important to understand that there are no *real* conflicts between the Bible and nature. As we know, God can't contradict Himself, and there can't be any contradiction between nature and the Bible because both are revelations from God.

So, where does the apparent conflict between science and the Bible exist? It is between the scientists' interpretation of nature and the theologians' interpretation of the Bible. Both science and the Bible have men and women who make mistakes when interpreting their data. The conflict lies in their fallible conclusions and not in the Bible and nature themselves. The war between the Bible and science is an *interpretive* one, not an actual one.

Following are some examples of the scientific knowledge the Bible displayed well ahead of its time:

1. The wind and water cycles (Ecclesiastes 1:6–7)
2. The laws of sanitation (Leviticus 13–15; Numbers 19)
3. The ocean floor containing mountains and valleys (Job 38:16; Psalm 18:15; Jonah 2:6)
4. The oceans having underwater springs (Genesis 7:11; Proverbs 8:28)

5. The earth having been created spherical or circular (round) (Isaiah 40:22)
6. The naming and workings of the constellations (Job 9:9; 38:31)
7. The laws of agriculture (Exodus 23:10–11)
8. The creation of man from dust (Genesis 2:7)
9. The beginning of the universe (Genesis 1:1)
10. The fact the universe is running down (Ps. 102:25–27)

There are many more examples that show the remarkable accuracy and consistency the Bible has with modern science.

The last point that will be made under this section is perhaps the most important: science can't be separated from the New Testament because Jesus often used scientific statements that are directly associated with Christian doctrine. For example, Jesus spoke regarding the doctrine of marriage by pointing out that God made humans in the beginning "male and female" (Matthew 19:1–4). This is a *biological* statement that can't be separated from His moral of marriage unless we do harm to the doctrine or to the scientific statement. This statement forms the foundation on which traditional marriage is to occur, namely between a man and a woman.

Can the Bible predict the future?

The Bible's ability to predict the future is one of the strongest reasons for believing its manuscripts are trustworthy. The ability to predict future events is called "prophecy." The role of a biblical prophet was not only to encourage and teach the people but also to predict future events in God's divine plan.

Bible prophecy is much different from the vague and obscure predictions of psychic readings, astrology, and fortune tellers, whose specific predictions are wrong the vast majority of the time. Biblical prophecy has a 100 percent *success* rate, while psychics, astrologers, and fortune tellers have a greater than 90 percent *failure* rate.[10] Knowing that, which do you trust?

The Bible contains a wealth of prophecies that were later fulfilled in the most minute detail. This amazing feature in Scripture demonstrates that God knows all and has complete control over past and future events (Isaiah 46:9–10; 48:3–5; 2 Peter 1:19–21). The following are several examples of detailed fulfilled prophecy:

1. Jesus was born in Bethlehem (Micah 5:2; compare Matthew 2:1).

2. Jesus was from the tribe of Judah (Genesis 49:10)

3. Jesus was a descendant of the house of David (Jeremiah 23:5; compare Luke 3:23, 31).

4. Jesus was born of a virgin woman (Isaiah 7:14; compare Matthew 1:18, 24–25).

5. Jesus entered Jerusalem riding a donkey (Zechariah 9:9; compare Luke 19:35–37).

6. Jesus was betrayed for thirty pieces of silver (Zechariah 11:12; compare Matthew 26:15).

7. Jesus was pierced (Zechariah 12:10; compare John 19:34).

8. Jesus was wounded and bruised for our sins (Isaiah 53:5; compare Matthew 27:26).

9. Jesus was smitten and spat upon (Isaiah 50:6; compare Matthew 26:67).

10. Jesus would be the cleanser of the temple (Malachi 3:1; compare Matthew 21:12f.).

11. Jesus would be rejected by Jews (Psalm 118:22; compare 1 Peter 2:7).

12. Jesus would die a humiliating death (Psalm 22 and Isaiah 53; compare Matthew 27:27f.).

13. Israel was reestablished as a nation (Ezekiel 36; occurred May 14, 1948).

14. Jesus raised from the dead (Psalms 2:7; 16:10; compare Acts 2:31 and Mark 16:6).

Jesus has personally fulfilled nearly two hundred prophecies. Many of the remaining prophecies concerning Jesus revolve around His second coming and the tribulation period. God has demonstrated His knowledge of all things and His complete command of the past, present, and future—proclaiming the end from the beginning (Isaiah 46:10). The prophetic character of Scripture as fulfilled in the New Testament indeed gives us good reason to believe it is worthy of our trust.

Review

1. Give three reasons why it is important to demonstrate the reliability of the New Testament.

(1) _____

_____

_____

(2) _____

_____

_____

(3) _____

_____

_____

2. What are manuscripts? Why are they an important piece of evidence to the trustworthiness of the New Testament?

_____

_____

_____

_____

_____

_____

3. What non-Christian sources could we use in showing unbelievers that the New Testament matches what historians say about the past? _____

_____

_____

_____

_____

_____

4. What function does archaeology play in proving the New Testament to be reliable? _____

_____

_____

_____

_____

_____

5. Why is the reliability of the New Testament a crucial link in demonstrating the deity of Christ and the divine origin of Scripture?

_____

_____

_____

_____

_____

_____

_____

6. What role does biblical prophecy play in showing the New Testament's reliability? _____

_____

_____

_____

_____

_____

_____

CHAPTER 10

Is Jesus God?

Scenario

One week later, Peter and Jordan are getting ready to play basketball in P.E. class.

Jordan: I haven't played basketball since last summer.

Peter: Neither have I, but I can't wait to start playing and hitting those jumpers. Swish!

Jordan: Yeah, right, you wish. Hey, I was thinking about all the evidence for the New Testament being trustworthy, so I went to the library and read part of a book that said Jesus is man. Then in another part it said Jesus is God. Sounds contradictory—which is He? God or man.

Peter: Well . . . uhh . . .

Questions

- Who was Jesus?
- What was Jesus?
- How would you describe Jesus to a nonbeliever?

Purpose

To provide an adequate understanding of Jesus' divine nature and His unique position within the Godhead

Goal

To apprehend the mystery surrounding the person of Christ and learn to communicate answers to objections that challenge Christ's divine nature

In this chapter we will learn

- that Jesus is God in human flesh.
- that the names and titles applied to the Father are also applied to Jesus.
- that Jesus possessed two distinct natures, one divine and the other human; both united in one person.
- the Trinity consists of three distinct persons (Father, Son, and Holy Spirit) united in one divine nature.
- that when God became man in Jesus Christ, He didn't subtract His divine nature, but, rather, He added a human nature.
- Jesus gave us good reason to believe He was God by the miracles He performed and His physical resurrection from the dead.
- the word *Son* in the phrase "Son of God" doesn't refer to Jesus as possessing a lesser nature than God, but rather to His function, position, or office He occupies within the Trinity.

The truth of Christianity rests with the truthfulness of Jesus Christ. Who is He? This chapter will offer various evidence to support that He was God in human flesh. Jesus' sinless and miraculous life, fulfillment of messianic prophecy (chap. 9), and bodily resurrection from the dead (chap. 11) provide the necessary evidence to support the claims about Him.

Many people have trouble accepting Jesus' radical claims to deity. Some are content simply going with the Christian program you have presented until Jesus is mentioned. Then an uncomfortable feeling creeps onto the scene, with your friends or teacher looking at you with disgust as if you had three heads and have just said something nerdy.

These awkward looks are from those who find it hard to accept the exclusive position of Christ in a world that believes all religious leaders have equal standing. This belief challenges the very heart of Christianity, namely, that Jesus is the unique Son of God (John 3:16).

Every Christian needs to think about effective ways to respond to those who find it hard to believe that Jesus holds an exclusive position apart from all others. Since we have already shown the New Testament to be a trustworthy record of the original writings (see chap. 9), the best place to begin is with what it says about Jesus.

Why is the deity of Christ important?

Throughout the centuries, there have been three major viewpoints on who Jesus is.

1. Jesus is God but not man.
2. Jesus is a good man but not God.
3. Jesus is fully God and fully man.

The third view is what Christians believe, namely, that Jesus is both God and man united in one person. It is important to realize that the identity of Jesus as both God and man is vitally related to the work He accomplished for us on the cross. In order for Jesus to be fully qualified to pay humanity's debt for sin, He had to be a man. This is because Jesus as a man could *represent* us (the guilty party) to God, even though Jesus Himself was without sin (Hebrews 4:15). In other words, because humankind had sinned, the payment must be paid by a human being (Jesus). In order for this "payment" or "sacrifice" to be satisfactory to God, it must be absolutely pure, without any stain of sin. This is why Jesus had to be God. There was no man alive on earth that met these strict qualifications (Romans 3:23). Only God Himself could take on the form of a man and offer Himself as the ultimate sinless sacrifice for our sin (John 3:16; Philippians 2:5–8). This would ensure that the sacrifice would be accepted by the Father and would have *infinite value*. This infinite value enabled Jesus' sacrifice to be applied in all ages and to all people who would receive it. The humanity and deity of Christ made Him the eternal Savior and Intercessor (1 Timothy 2:5; Titus 2:13; Hebrews 7:25).

What does the Bible say about who Jesus is?

The Bible reveals many statements about Jesus' identity and His special relationship to His Father (Jehovah). The following chart will show that the exclusive names and titles that are applied to the Father are also applied to the Son (Jesus). This indicates the Father and the Son's common identity as God.[1]

Jesus is
the *shepherd* (John 10:11)
the *I AM* (John 8:24, 58;
    13:19)
the *creator* (John 1:3;
    Colossians 1:15–17)
the *first and the last*
    (Revelation 1:17)
God (John 1:1; 20:28;
    Titus 2:13; Hebrews 1:8)
the *savior* (Acts 4:12;
    Romans 10:9)
the *forgiver* of sins
    (Mark 2:7, 10)
addressed in prayer (Acts 7:59)
confessed as Lord
    (Philippians 2:10)
worshiped by angels
    (Hebrews 1:6)
worshiped by men
    (Matthew 14:31–33)
unchanging (Hebrews 13:8)
eternal (John 8:58;
    Hebrews 13:8)
all-knowing (John 2:24–25;
    John 4:16–19)
present everywhere
    (Matthew 18:20)
all-powerful (Colossians 2:10;
    Matthew 28:18)

The Father is
the *shepherd* (Psalm 23:1)
the *I AM* (Exodus 3:14;
    Isaiah 43:10)
the *creator* (Genesis 1:1;
    Isaiah 40:22, 28)
the *first and the last* (Isaiah 44:6)

God (Isaiah 43:10; 45:22)

savior (Isaiah 45:21; 43:3, 11)

the *forgiver* of sins
    (Jeremiah 31:34)
addressed in prayer (Daniel 6)
confessed as Lord (Psalm 34:3;
    Isaiah 45:23)
worshiped by angels (Psalm 148:2)

worshiped by men (Exodus 34:14)

unchanging (Malachi 3:6)
eternal (Deuteronomy 33:27)

all-knowing (Psalm 139:1–6;
    1 John 3:20)
present everywhere
    (Psalm 139:7–12)
all-powerful
    (Psalm 139:13–24)[2]

Did Jesus claim to be God?

Central to Christianity is the belief that Jesus is God manifest in human flesh. Justification for this crucial belief is found in what Jesus said and how others responded to Him. The implications that follow from His claims and deeds are unmistakably clear: Jesus is God. The following are conditions and claims unique to God alone.

1. Jesus claimed to be equal with God (John 5:22–23, 26–29; Mark 2:5–7; compare Jeremiah 31:34).
2. Jesus spoke as Jehovah (Zechariah 12:10; compare John 19:37).
3. Jesus gives life to whomever He pleases, just as the Father gives life to whomever He pleases (John 5:21).
4. Jesus was called God by the apostle John and the apostle Paul (John 1:1, 14; Titus 1:3; 2:13).
5. Jesus asserted He was one with the Father (John 10:30–33; 14:7).
6. Jesus applied to Himself titles reserved only for Jehovah (Revelation 1:17; compare Isaiah 42:8; John 10:11; compare Psalms 23:1; Matthew 25:37f.; John 5:27; compare Joel 3:12).
7. Jesus declared He was the "I AM" applied to Jehovah (John 8:58; compare Exodus 3:14).
8. Jesus accepted worship and said He is to be given the same honor *and* reverence accorded to the Father (Matthew 14:31–33; 28:16–17; John 5:23; 9:38; Hebrews 1:6; compare Deuteronomy 6:13; 10:20; Exodus 34:14; Matthew 4:10).
9. Jesus said He was the Messiah (who is God) (John 4:25–26; compare Psalm 110:1–2; Isaiah 9:6; Zechariah 12:10; Micah 5:2).
10. Jesus claimed to possess the glory of God (John 17:4–5; Matthew 17:1–5; compare Isaiah 42:8).
11. Jesus was prayed to by Stephen while being stoned to death (Acts 7:59–60).
12. Jesus claimed to be omnipresent, omnipotent, and omniscient, which are attributes of God alone (Matthew 28:18, 20; John 2:25; 4:18; 16:30; compare Matthew 16:21; John 14:23; Ephesians 3:17; Colossians 1:27).
13. Jesus was acknowledged as the Savior of the world (Matthew 26:63–64; Mark 14:61–62; John 4:42; compare Isaiah 43:3; Titus 2:13).
14. Thomas declared that Jesus was both Lord and God (John 20:28; Titus 2:13).

How can Jesus be both God and man?

After reviewing the chart above with all the names and titles associated with Jesus, there can be little doubt about the scriptural position on Christ's divine nature. Nonetheless, there remain those passages in the Bible that certainly portray Jesus as a human man. After all, Jesus became tired and needed rest (John 4:6), became thirsty (John 4:7), wept (John 11:34–35), and slept (Mark 4:38). He also grew in wisdom and knowledge (Luke 2:52) and even experienced temptation in all points as we have (Matthew 4:4–10; Hebrews 4:15). Jesus also died on the cross (John 19).

This may bring to mind several questions. How can God—who is perfect in all wisdom, knowledge, and power—need all the things that Jesus needed to survive? Can God die? If God is perfect, why did Jesus need anything?

The portions of Scripture that *seem* to be at odds with Jesus' divine nature are not really problems at all. When we realize that Jesus had *two different natures* united in *one person*, our confusion disappears. One of Jesus' natures was human and the other was divine (further explanation follows in this chapter).

Throughout Jesus' ministry He operated either from His divine nature or His human nature depending, on the will of God at that particular time (John 5). It is important to remember that Jesus' two natures (divine and human) are not mixed together like a milk shake, nor are they separated like railroad tracks. They are touching one another just as the triangle and the circle below touch each other while remaining *distinct*. Just as a triangle possesses three distinct points and one triangular nature, so also does the Trinity possess three distinct persons and one divine nature or essence. The circle represents Christ's human nature.

The following diagram illustrates Christ's two natures united in one person: the Son.

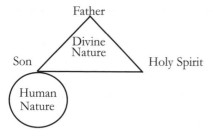

While reviewing the diagram, we can see that the incarnation of Christ is no more contradictory than simply adding a circle to a triangle. Keep in mind that whenever we speak about Jesus we must always ask two questions about Him: one question about His *divine nature* (triangle) and the other about His *human nature* (circle). For example, if someone were to ask about whether Jesus became tired, we would answer that in His humanity "yes" but in His deity "no." How about the question of whether Jesus knew all things. The same would apply: Jesus knew all things in His deity (John 1:47–51; 2:24–25) but not in His humanity (Luke 2:52).

Some people would like to think that the Son of God laid aside His divine nature when He came to earth in the form of the man Jesus. This view is incorrect because the Son did not discard His divine nature; He simply took on a human nature. Philippians 2:5–7 reads: "Let this mind be in you which was also in Christ Jesus, who, being in the form of God, did not consider it robbery to be equal with God, but made Himself of no reputation, taking the form of a bondservant, and coming in the likeness of men."

We can be assured that God did not throw off His divine nature. Malachi 3:6 says that the nature of God cannot change. The Son merely added humanity; He didn't change or subtract His deity in the process. While this is a mystery that goes *beyond* our ability to comprehend (Romans 11:33–36), it doesn't go *contrary* to our ability to apprehend this marvelous truth. God provided a qualified sacrifice that could identify with our weaknesses and yet still be powerful enough to save us from sin.

If the Father, the Son, and the Holy Spirit are God, do we have three Gods?

Even though the Father, the Son, and the Holy Spirit are God (John 8:58; 10:30; Titus 2:13; Acts 5:1–4), Christians do not worship three gods (tritheism). Some become confused at this point, but this need not be the case. Just remember that there are *three* distinct persons (Father, Son, Holy Spirit) within *one* divine nature. This unique relationship within the Godhead is known as the Trinity.

The Trinity of God is an important part of the Christian faith. At first glance it may sound like a contradiction (three-in-one?). To make clear our understanding of the Trinity, we must be aware of the difference between *person* and *nature*. Person is *who* you are, and nature is *what* you are. For example, each of us possesses an individual identity and personality unique to ourselves. This is "who" we are as individuals. However, we also have a nature, which is human in kind. This is "what" we are. Who and what we are can exist within one being. This is similar to how the Trinity exists, except there are three distinct *who's* (persons) with one *what* (divine nature). The following diagram may help explain the Trinity.

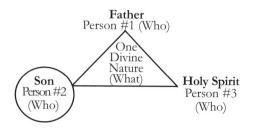

The triangle helps us to gain a clearer understanding of the Trinity in that each of the three points represents the persons (who) within the Trinity. The Trinity is no more contradictory than one triangle with three sides. There are three distinct corners in one triangle. It illustrates the Godhead as three united persons without separate existence. The inside body of the triangle represents God's divine nature (what He is). Just as it is reasonable to believe one triangle has three sides, so also is the belief in one God with three persons (Father, Son, and Holy Spirit). Even though our minds can't fully *comprehend* the inner workings of God (Romans 11:33–36), we can at least *apprehend* the idea. If we try to fully comprehend the infinite nature of the Trinity, we may loose our minds; however, if we do not apprehend it, we may loose our souls.

Does "Son of God" mean Jesus is a lesser being than the Father?

When we read of Jesus being called the "Son of God," we may question whether Jesus is equal or inferior to God. We immediately think of a human father-and-son relationship and the differences that accompany such a relationship. How can a son be equal to his father? Very simply, the son is equal to the father in *nature* (both are equally human), but they are different in *position* (the father is in a higher position than is the son). This can be explained by looking at the phrase more closely and noticing how the writers of the Bible use it in other passages. Let's first look at the phrase itself.

Son of God

The first two words—*Son of*—refers to Jesus' position or function in relation to the Father. It is important to remember that Christ's Sonship is different from a human sonship in that it is not physically acquired through normal sexual relations between a husband and wife. Jesus' sonship is eternal! This means that Jesus' position as the Son of God is not biological but relational. There was never a time when Jesus was not the Son of God (Proverbs 30:4; John 3:16–17; 8:54–58; Colossians 1:13–17). Granted, Jesus was conceived by the Holy Spirit and born nine months later; yet, it was not His *divine* nature that was born, it was His *human* nature. The word *of* in this phrase literally means "of the order of." Although "son of" can refer to the "offspring of" humans in some instances, it can also be used to indicate the sameness of nature and the equality of being. This means that the phrase "Son of God" literally means the position of Christ as a Son is after the order or nature of God. This is a claim to deity. In other words, Christ is equal to the Father in deity but lesser in function (John 5:18; 10:33).

Even the Jews who were attempting to trap Jesus understood the phrase "Son of God" to mean that Jesus was claiming equality with God (see John 5:18; 19:7). This equality in nature and difference in function is similar to a man and woman being the same in nature (both are equally human) yet having different functions within God's established order within the home—the man being the head of the wife, Christ being the head of the man, and God being the head of Christ (1 Corinthians 11:3). You and I are no more or less human than the president of the United States even though the president has a greater function, position, or office. We are all equally human. In the same sense, Jesus is equally God even though the Father's position or function is greater than the Son's.[3]

Jesus is equal to the Father in	The Father is greater than Jesus in
essence	function
nature	office
character	position
divine substance	relationship[4]

It is clear that the phrase refers to Christ's deity and in no way lowers Christ to a lesser kind of existence. There is only a difference in *position, function, office,* and *relationship* within the order of the Trinity.

Do we have proof that Jesus is God?

Absolutely! Jesus' claim to be God is one of the most heavily supported claims in ancient history. There are three lines of evidence that demonstrate Jesus is who He said He was.

First, there is confirmation of Jesus' claims to deity by His sinless and miraculous life. The sinless and righteous character of Christ's life is a momentous accomplishment in itself. Several times throughout the New Testament Jesus' enemies brought accusations against Him. However, both friends and enemies eventually confessed their agreement with the sinless nature of Jesus.

1. At the trial of Jesus, Pontius Pilate said, "I find no fault in this Man" (Luke 23:4).
2. The Roman soldier at the crucifixion said, "Certainly this was a righteous man!" (Luke 23:47).
3. The thief on the cross next to Jesus asserted, "This Man has done nothing wrong" (Luke 23:41).
4. Judas spoke of Jesus when he declared, "I have sinned by betraying innocent blood" (Matthew 27:4).
5. Peter called Jesus "a lamb without blemish and without spot" (1 Peter 1:19).
6. Peter also said, "Nor was deceit found in His mouth" (1 Peter 2:22).
7. John called Jesus "righteous" (1 John 2:1; compare 3:7).
8. Paul expressed that Christ "knew no sin" (2 Corinthians 5:21).
9. The writer of Hebrews says that Christ was "without sin" (Hebrews 4:15).
10. Even Jesus asked His accusers, "Which of you convicts Me of sin?" (John 8:46).

At this point, confusion often arises due to the competition that exists between verses in the Bible that claim that Jesus was "made . . . to be sin for us" (2 Corinthians 5:21) and those that say Jesus was "without sin" (Hebrews 4:15). But how can Jesus be both made sin and without sin? It is important to remember that this problem can be solved by distinguishing Jesus' *personal acts* from His *substitutionary role*. A substitute is one who stands in for another. This means Jesus was not guilty of any sin *personally* but was made to be sin *substitutionally*. That is, by His death on the cross He paid the penalty for our sins, thereby erasing the penalty of sin against us. Jesus was made to be sin *judicially* for us but not actually in Himself.

Christ was not sinful	Christ was made to be sin
in Himself	for us
personally	substitutionally
actually	judicially[5]

Beyond the moral aspects of Jesus' sinless life, the miraculous nature of His ministry is evidential as well. As we have seen in chapter 8, miracles are acts of God that confirm the truth of God associated with them.[6] Jesus' accomplishment of what is humanly impossible gives us good reason to believe that what He said about Himself is true. Unlike many other religious leaders who make empty claims about themselves, Jesus left us proof through His actions. He healed the sick, raised the dead, displayed power over nature, and walked on water, all of which were confirmed by eyewitnesses (Luke 1:1–4; John 19:35; 20:30; 1 Corinthians 15:6–8). Notice the important confirming role miracles play in the following verses.

- "'But *that you may know* that the Son of Man has power on earth to forgive sins'—He said to the paralytic, 'I say to you, arise, take up your bed, and go to your house'" (Mark 2:10–11, emphasis added).
- "There was a man of the Pharisees named Nicodemus, a ruler of the Jews. This man came to Jesus by night and said to Him, 'Rabbi, we know that You are a teacher come from God; for *no one can do these signs that You do unless God is with him*'" (John 3:1–2, emphasis added).
- "He also presented Himself alive after His suffering by many infallible proofs, being seen by them during forty days" (Acts 1:3).
- Peter said, "Men of Israel, hear these words: Jesus of Nazareth, a Man attested by God to you by miracles, wonders, and signs which God did through Him in your midst" (Acts 2:22).
- "How shall we escape if we neglect so great a salvation, which at the first began to be spoken by the Lord, and was confirmed to us by those who heard Him, God also bearing witness both with signs and wonders, with various miracles, and gifts of the Holy Spirit, according to His own will?" (Hebrews 2:3, emphasis added).

The major difference between Jesus and Buddha, Confucius, Muhammad, and Hare Krishna is that Jesus gave us every indication through His miracles that what He said was true. Through those same signs and wonders He also gave us evidence that He had the *power* to fulfill His promises. No other religious leader has come close to giving humankind the kind of supernatural signs that Jesus did. Even though the Qur'an of Muslims acknowledges that prophets before Muhammad, including Jesus, did miracles to confirm their claim to speak for God, yet Muhammad refused to do the same when challenged (Sura 3:183; 17:102).

The second proof Jesus gave us that He is God was His fulfillment of messianic prophecy (see chap. 9). By Christ's fulfillment of hundreds of prophecies, He stands alone when it comes to the believability of His claims to be God (John 5:17–18; 8:58; 9:35–38).

The third proof that confirms Jesus' claim to be God is His physical resurrection from the dead. This proof is the crowning evidence that catapults Jesus and Christianity to the front of the line. Only someone who has power over life and death could accomplish such a miracle. The Resurrection is of such importance that if it crumbles, all of Christianity crumbles with it. Since this third proof is of crucial importance, the next chapter will be dedicated entirely to this topic.

Conclusion

There is no doubt Jesus made extraordinary claims. He said, "I am the way, the truth, and the life. No one comes to the Father except through Me" (John 14:6) and "Before Abraham was, I am" (John 8:58). These are claims that leave no room for guesswork as to whom Jesus really is. Either He is God in human flesh *or* He was a liar, legend, or lunatic. No other religious leader lived a sinless and miraculous life and displayed the love for people by dying on the cross for the sins of the world (Romans 5:6–8). The eyewitness testimony of His miracles, prophecy, and resurrection from the dead are more than any court jury would ever need to render a sound verdict.[7] Jesus is Lord!

Review

1. Does the Bible portray Jesus as man, God, or both?

_____

_____

2. How could Jesus be both God and man?

_____

_____

_____

3. If Jesus is God, how do we explain when He became tired, hungry, and thirsty like any other human being?

_____

_____

_____

4. What does the phrase "Son of God" mean?

_____

_____

_____

5. In what way is the Father greater than the Son?

_____

_____

_____

_____

6. List several proofs Jesus gave us to prove that He is God. ___

_____

_____

_____

_____

7. Read John 1:1–14 and Philippians 2:5–11 and then summarize what the two passages say about Jesus.

_____

_____

_____

_____

CHAPTER 11

Did Jesus Rise from the Dead?

Scenario

Jordan and Sarah joined Peter and Jennifer for the Easter morning service. After church, they grabbed some tacos and went to the beach. While there Sarah and Jordan ask about the preacher's sermon.

Sarah: That was an interesting sermon. I didn't know that there were so many people interested in Jesus' resurrection.

Jordan: I wonder if Jesus really rose from the dead. Peter, do you believe it, really?

Peter: Yes, I— *(Sarah interrupts.)*

Sarah: My dad said there is no proof for the Resurrection. I can't blame him. I mean, have any of you seen a dead person live again?

Jennifer: No, but I haven't seen Abraham Lincoln either, and I believe he existed.

Jordan: I never thought of that. Why do you believe Jesus rose from the dead, Jennifer? Why does it matter anyway?

Jennifer: Uhhh . . . good question.

Questions

- Why is Jesus' resurrection so important to your faith?
- What facts do you know about the Resurrection and the period immediately following it?
- Did Jesus rise from the dead?

Purpose

To show the importance of Jesus' bodily resurrection as a historical event and how it helps prove that Jesus was God

Goal

To understand the evidence surrounding the bodily resurrection and be able to provide answers to theories that challenge this important miraculous event

In this chapter we will learn

- that Jesus rose from the tomb in the same body in which He died on the cross, yet there were changes in it.
- that the word *resurrection* refers to the time when the same body that died will again rise from the grave to be rejoined with your spirit.
- that a *resurrection* is different from a *resuscitation*
- that a *resurrection* is a change *in* body and *reincarnation* is a change *of* body.
- that there is abundant eyewitness *evidence* to support Jesus' resurrection.
- that challenges against Jesus' bodily resurrection are flawed for several reasons.

The resurrection of Jesus Christ is the crucial event that serves as the crowning apologetic of Christianity. Christianity stands or falls with the resurrection of Christ. It is the very foundation upon which the Christian faith is built (1 Corinthians 15:1–8; Ephesians 2:19–22; Romans 10:9–10) and without the resurrection there would be no Christianity (Romans 4:25; 1 Corinthians 15:12–19). This special event not only confirms what Jesus taught (Hebrews 2:3–4; Matthew 12:40–41), but who He is—God (Romans 1:4).

The Resurrection event also elevated early Christianity above the other religions of that same time period, and it continues presently to position the Christian faith above competing world religions. Still, the Resurrection is not without its skeptics. One would expect attacks from the unbelieving world, but when these assaults come from within the church, they stand to overthrow the faith of some, while others are prevented from coming to the knowledge of the truth. Many of these false doctrines are a result of simple misunderstandings, while others come from disbelief. It is for this reason we will address several areas of importance.

What is a resurrection?

The Greek word for *resurrection (anastasis),* which is derived from another Greek word *(anistemi),* literally means "to stand up." So, when Christians speak of the resurrection, they are referring to a time when the same body that died will again "stand up" or "rise" from the grave, never to die again (1 Corinthians 15) or be subjected to pain and death (John 5:28–29; Revelation 21:4). It is different from a resuscitation, such as when Jesus raised Lazarus from the dead in John 11. A resurrection is more than a resuscitation in quality (kind of life) and quantity (length of life). A resuscitated body will again be subjected to pain and death; a resurrected body will not. It is imperishable and immortal, not perishable and mortal (see 1 Corinthians 15:35–53).

Our resurrected bodies will possess the following characteristics:

1. It will be a physical body (Luke 24:39; John 20:27–29, compare John 2:19 and 1 John 3:2).

2. It will be the same physical body (Luke 24:39; John 2:19) as before death, except with changes (1 Corinthians 15:51–52; 37–38).

3. Mortality will put on immortality (1 Corinthians 15:54).

4. The corruptible will be changed to incorruptible (1 Corinthians 15:50–53).

5. It will die in dishonor; it will be raised in glory (1 Corinthians 15:43).

6. It will die in weakness; it will be raised in power (1 Corinthians 15:43).

7. It will die a natural body; it will be raised in a spirit dominated body (1 Corinthians 15:44; compare 10:1–4).

(Note: These characteristics will be further explained throughout this chapter.)

What about reincarnation?

A resurrection is much different from a reincarnation. The word *reincarnation* literally means "again in the flesh." Many Eastern religious systems such as Buddhism and Hinduism, as well as the New Age Movement, believe that when people die their spirit will again be born into the world in another body. This new body may take the form of a human being, animal, vegetable, or mineral, depending on which form of reincarnation one believes. The ultimate goal of the reincarnationist is to free or release his or her spirit from the cycle of rebirths (reincarnations) and become one with God. To accomplish this freedom, one must be sure to use maximum effort in living a good and spiritual life in the present existence. In other words, reincarnation is a kind of spiritual evolution into godhood.

Many Christians are lured into believing that a resurrection and a reincarnation are the same thing; however, they are not. For the Christian, belief in the resurrection of Jesus is essential for salvation. Romans 10:9–10 says, "If you confess with your mouth the Lord Jesus and believe in your heart that God raised Him from the dead, you will be saved." Indeed, the Resurrection is at the heart of the gospel message (1 Corinthians 15:1–11).

There are at least three important reasons why a belief in Christ's physical bodily resurrection is necessary. First, someone who is dead can't save anyone. Forgiveness and eternal life can only be guaranteed and given by someone who is alive. Second, someone who has not conquered death cannot help us overcome it (John 14:19). Third, if Jesus hadn't been raised from the dead in the same body in which He died, then Satan won the battle. Jesus' body would still be in the grave, allowing death to have the victory (Acts 2:22–36). Fourth, our faith is only as good as the person in whom we believe. If our belief is based on Jesus' power to raise us from the dead, and Jesus doesn't have that power, then we have an empty faith and can't look forward to conquering death. For example, if we had faith in a wooden chair to write a theater play, and the chair can't write, our faith is in vain. Our faith is only as good as its object (the chair). It is the same with faith in Jesus.

It is interesting that Jesus was raised from the dead in His body. This should be very comforting to us, knowing that God sent His Son to save the whole person, both spirit and body (Romans 8:11, 23). This gives us good reason to believe that God not only cares about our spiritual life but also our physical needs. This issue separates reincarnation from resurrection. Many reincarnationists view the body as a hinderance or nuisance to spirituality. Christians, on the other hand, believe the body and spirit form the whole person, and the union is a gift than can be used to glorify God in worship and good deeds. In other words, whereas a reincarnated body is viewed as a problem, a resurrected body is viewed as a precious gift from God. The following characteristics distinguish the two views.[1]

1. A resurrected body is in its final glorified condition never to experience death again (Hebrews 9:27).

A reincarnated body is just another mortal body that will die again.

2. A resurrection is a change *in* body (1 Corinthians 15:51–53). You are the same human person.

A reincarnation is a change *of* body. You may be a different person or animal next time.

3. A resurrected body is heavenly and supernatural (1 Corinthians 15:44).

A reincarnated body is earthly and natural.

4. A resurrected body is viewed by Christians as a gift from God (1 Corinthians 15:54–57).

A reincarnated body is viewed by reincarnationists as a problem or hinderance to spirituality.

5. A resurrected body is viewed by Christians as involving the *salvation* of the *whole person,* both body and spirit.

Being delivered from a reincarnated body is viewed by reincarnationists as a way to *free the spirit* from the body in order to become one with God.

When evaluating reincarnation, several problems emerge with accepting it as a true view of the afterlife.

First, reincarnation is unproven. There is no evidence that life begins prior to the very first sign of pregnancy. In fact, scientific experts have shown that life begins when the male sperm joins with the female egg. The reincarnationists try to support their view by pointing out that there have been people who have "recalled" or "remembered" their past lives. However, usually they have been taught to believe they once lived in the distant past. Most often, this "teaching" was done through hypnotism or some other mind-altering technique or through suggestive counseling. Further, many of the events described by reincarnationists of their past life have been shown to be false and to have never occurred.[2]

Second, reincarnation hinders compassion. A key concept behind traditional reincarnation is the belief that the present condition of one's life, such as being rich, poor, starving, handicapped, or under-privileged, is a direct result of the person's previous life. Any attempt by another to help someone who is suffering is discouraged because the one suffering is "paying" for the wrongs committed in the last life. As soon as he is done "paying" for his "debt," he will progress to a higher level. This has led to the belief that every person is on his own when attempting to gain salvation (release from reincarnation). This is much different from Jesus' command to love each other as we love ourselves (Proverbs 28:27; Matthew 5:43–48; 22:39) and to receive the gift of salvation freely (Ephesians 2:8–9).

Did the resurrection of Jesus actually occur?

In showing that the resurrection of Jesus was an event that really occurred in history, we again look to reliable reports from those who were there to see it (eyewitnesses). Consider the following five important points.

1. The authors of the Gospels (Matthew, Mark, Luke, and John) claimed to have been either actual eyewitnesses or to have gathered firsthand information by speaking with those who had seen the events (Luke 1:1–3; 3:1; John 15:27; 19:35; 21:24; Acts 2:22; 26:24–26; 2 Peter 1:16; 1 John 1:3).

2. No written evidence from anyone in the first century speaks *against* the Gospel reports of the Resurrection. Yet, as has been demonstrated, historians such as Tacitus, Seutonius, and Josephus provide abundant testimony that matches the Gospel records of Jesus' life, death, and resurrection.

3. If the New Testament picture of Jesus were not based on eyewitness reports, how could a consistent report about Him ever have been formed and written? All individuals would have their own versions of what happened. Just the opposite is true because we have a remarkably consistent record of the biblical events.

4. To believe that the Gospels were not written by good eyewitnesses leaves several questions unanswered. For example, how could the apostles have succeeded in Jerusalem if the message of Jesus they presented was untrue? Why would they have begun there in the first place? The citizens of that area would have quickly exposed the disciples' lies.

5. Christ's resurrection was confirmed by several eyewitnesses who saw Jesus' body alive after He died and was buried (Acts 1:3).

(1) Mary Magdalene (John 20:1)

(2) Mary the mother of James (Matthew 28:1)

(3) Salome and Joanna (Luke 24:10)

(4) Several other women from Galilee (Luke 23:55)

(5) Peter (Luke 24:34)

(6) Cleopas and the other disciple on the road to Emmaus (Luke 24:13–32)

(7) The ten apostles in Jerusalem (John 20:24)

(8) The eleven, when Thomas was present a week later (John 20:26–29)

(9) The seven disciples on the Sea of Galilee (John 21:1–24)

(10) The eleven on the mountain in Galilee (Matthew 28:16–20)

(11) The five hundred at one time (1 Corinthians 15:6)

(12) Jesus' brother James (1 Corinthians 15:7a)

(13) The disciples on the Mount of Olives (Acts 1:4–12)

(14) The apostle Paul (1 Corinthians 15:7; 9:1)

If one chooses to reject the eyewitness testimony of Christ's resurrection, he must also reject the eyewitness testimony of most ancient events. This is because there is more eyewitness testimony for the resurrection of Jesus than for other events of the same time period.

Do the Gospels provide evidence of the Resurrection?

Not only was there an overwhelming number of eyewitnesses to the events described in the Gospels, the nature of their reports place the Resurrection beyond suspicion. Several factors indicate this.

First, the witnesses were in most cases independent of each other, with the first thirteen appearances occurring over forty days (Acts 1:3). This shows us that they were not joining together to lie about the Resurrection.

Second, there was initial disbelief in what the witnesses saw, which would eliminate the possibility of hallucination (compare John 20:25 f.; Luke 24:15 f.; Matthew 28:17 f.). Usually people who want to believe in something hallucinate about it, but the disciples did not believe Jesus was going to rise.

Third, the different perspectives of Matthew, Mark, Luke, and John strongly suggest that the witnesses were telling the truth. If they were copying each other, their accounts would be almost identical. Further, the apostles' truthfulness and moral character are reflected in their writings. They did not tolerate lying (Acts 5:1 f.), they refused to be bought with money (Acts 8:18), and they remained steadfast in their testimony when facing persecution (2 Corinthians 11:23 f.), even to the point of death.

In light of the evidence for the Gospels being written by those who were eyewitnesses of the events, combined with the evidence for the character of the witnesses, it is reasonable to believe that the Gospels accurately recorded the truth.

How do skeptics explain the Resurrection?

There are a number of different theories that have emerged over the years in an attempt to explain away the facts that surround Jesus' resurrection. The following are some of the more popular skeptical theories that challenge Christianity.[3]

Jesus didn't really die; He fainted

According to this view, Jesus did not actually die on the cross, but rather swooned, fainted, or feigned death by a drug-induced condition. Jesus was then said to have later revived in the cool, damp tomb until He was strong enough to leave.

Problems with this view:

1. It fails to consider the extent of Jesus' physical condition.
   a. He had no sleep the night before the crucifixion (Mark 14:32–41).
   b. He could not bear the weight of the cross (Matthew 27:32).
   c. He was scourged, mocked, and beaten (Matthew 26:27–28; 27:26–31).
   d. His hands and feet had been nailed to the cross (Luke 24:39).
   e. His side had been pierced by a spear (John 19:34).
   f. He had hung on the cross from 9:00 A.M. until at least 3:00 P.M. (Mark 15:25, 33–34).
   g. In 1986, medical scholars evaluated the wounds that were absorbed by Jesus and wrote: "Clearly, the weight of historical and medical evidence indicates that Jesus was dead before the wound to his side was inflicted and supports

the traditional view that the spear, thrust between his right ribs, probably perforated not only the right lung but also the pericardium and heart and thereby ensured his death. Accordingly, interpretations based on the assumption that Jesus did not die on the cross appear to be at odds with modern medical knowledge."[4]

2. It fails to consider those who were witnesses of His death.
   a. Pilate ordered his soldiers to check and make sure Jesus was dead before burial (Mark 15:44–45).
   b. The Roman soldiers pronounced Jesus dead (John 19:33–34).
   c. Jesus was embalmed and wrapped with nearly one hundred pounds of material (John 19:39–40).
   d. A heavy stone was rolled in front of the tomb (John 20:1).
   e. The apostle John witnessed Jesus' death (John 19:30).

3. It fails to consider non-Christian testimony written by historians who recorded Jesus' death.[5]
   a. Roman historian Tacitus asserts that "their originator, Christ, had been executed in Tiberius' reign by the governor of Judaea, Pontius Pilatus."[6]
   b. Josephus makes reference to Jesus being handed over to "Pilate" and later being "condemned to the cross."[7]
   c. The Talmud (book on Jewish tradition and history) records "on the eve of Passover, Yeshua was hanged."[8]
   d. In the second century, Lucian documents Jesus' death when he writes, "The Christians, you know, worship a *man* to this day—the distinguished personage who introduced their novel rites, and was crucified on that account."[9]

The witnesses only thought they had seen Jesus alive

According to this theory, those who reported seeing Jesus after His death were actually not seeing correctly but, rather, were hallucinating and probably seeing what they wanted to see.

Problems with this theory:

1. It fails to consider the abundant number of witnesses. Hallucinations are usually private and individual.
   a. Christ appeared to more than five hundred people (1 Corinthians 15:3–8) at the same time and place.
   b. He appeared to all the apostles at once (Acts 1:4–8).

2. It fails to consider that hallucinations usually occur once and only last a few seconds or minutes—rarely hours.

    a. If Christ was a hallucination, it would be the longest recorded one in history (forty days) (Acts 1:3).

    b. Jesus appeared for prolonged periods of time and held extended conversations (John 21:3–23).

3. It fails to consider that the disciples touched Him and ate with Him.

    a. He showed Himself to "Doubting" Thomas (John 20:26–30).

    b. He showed the disciples His hands and feet (Luke 24:39).

    c. He ate broiled fish with the disciples (Luke 24:43).

4. This theory fails to give an answer for why there was an empty tomb.

5. If the apostles were hallucinating and spreading their story contrary to fact, the Jewish and Roman authorities could have easily stopped the uprising by producing the body of Jesus.

There was a criminal plot behind the missing body

According to this theory, either the Jewish authorities, the Roman guards, or the disciples conspired to steal the body of Jesus.

Problems with this theory:

1. If Jewish authorities stole the body, why didn't they charge the disciples with the theft or produce the body to discredit the early church witnesses to the Resurrection?

2. The Roman guards wouldn't have taken the body for fear of the death penalty. Besides it is unlikely that the Romans had a reason for stealing the body. They wouldn't have stolen it because it would have been counterproductive for maintaining peace in the region since it would have caused a controversy.

3. The disciples didn't steal the body because they later died for what they confessed to be true (i.e., the Resurrection). Indeed, people do die for what they have been deceived into thinking is the truth, but they do not die for what they know to be a lie.

4. This theory portrays the disciples as schemers who desired to capitalize on the situation. This is contrary to both their teachings and the high moral character for which they were known.

5. It doesn't account for the twelve appearances of Christ to more than five hundred people over a span of forty days.

The witnesses went to the wrong gravesite

According to this view, Mary Magdalene and the other women went to the wrong tomb and discovered it empty. Those who hold this view believe that early morning darkness, emotional distress, and wishful thinking accounted for this mistake.[10]

Problems with this theory:

1. If Mary went to the wrong tomb because it was dark, the authorities could have found the right tomb in the daylight. Peter and John did successfully find the right tomb (John 20:1–5).

2. If it was so dark that Mary couldn't see, why was the gardener already working? Gardeners rarely work before dawn.

3. This theory does not account for the many appearances of Christ or for the empty tomb.

Was the resurrected body of Jesus material or immaterial?

Some believe Jesus received an invisible "spirit body" because of what the apostle Paul wrote in 1 Corinthians 15:44, that the body is "sown a *natural body,* it is raised a *spiritual body.* There is a natural body, and there is a *spiritual body*" (emphasis added). Even though this verse may seem to support the idea that the resurrection body is invisible, at closer look it reveals that Paul is talking about a physical body dominated by the Spirit, which he calls a "spiritual body." There are several reasons why most conservative Bible scholars believe this to be true.

First, just because something is "spiritual," doesn't mean it's immaterial. Paul writes in 1 Corinthians 10:4 that there was "spiritual food," "spiritual drink," and a "spiritual rock" that the children of Israel ate and drank from in the wilderness. These things were real, not invisible. Just because they were called spiritual does not mean they were invisible. Neither does Paul's use of the term *spiritual* concerning the resurrected body mean that it is invisible or immaterial. Spirituality does not mean immateriality.

Second, we would call the apostles spiritual men and the Bible a spiritual book; however, we would not assume that the apostles were invisible or that the Bible is immaterial. It simply means that the apostles lives were characterized by the supernatural power of the Holy Spirit and that the Bible is a supernatural book possessing a spiritual source. Therefore, when Paul says our resurrection body will be a "spiritual body," he is referring to the supernatural source it will possess, not an invisible substance. It would be accurate to say that we will receive a "supernatural body" dominated by the Holy Spirit.

Third, the Greek word for *body* (*soma*) that Paul uses always refers to a real material body when applied to persons, never an immaterial one.[11]

Fourth, if God didn't raise Jesus in the same physical body in which He died, then the Resurrection is unimpressive as a proof for the truthfulness of Christianity and God's power over death. This is because there is no way to empirically verify a "spiritual resurrection." In fact, there is no verifiable difference between a spiritual resurrection and no resurrection at all because neither can be examined. Moreover, if Christ simply received another invisible body that could appear on occasion, then God lost the battle with death and the grave because Jesus' original body would still be in the tomb. However, we know Jesus rose from the grave in the same body in which He died because Peter said it was not possible that Jesus could be held by the pains of death (Acts 2:22–24), nor would His body see corruption (Acts 2:31). This is why Scripture boldly says, "Death is swallowed up in victory. O Death, where is your sting? O Hades, where is your victory?" (1 Corinthians 15:54–55).

There are several other reasons why Christians believe that Jesus' body was material.

1. Jesus' body was physically recognized (Matthew 28:7, 17; Mark 16:7; Luke 24:24; John 20:14, 20; 1 Corinthians 9:1).

2. Jesus' body was physically touched and offered to be touched (Matthew 28:9; John 20:17, 27).

3. Jesus ate physical food (Luke 24:30, 41–43; John 21:12–13).

4. His body was made of "flesh and bones" (Luke 24:39).

5. It was seen and heard with physical senses (Matthew 28:17; Luke 24:31; 1 Corinthians 9:1; 15:5–8).

6. Jesus' body will be recognized at the second coming (Revelation 1:7; Acts 1:11).

7. Jesus' tomb was empty of His physical body that had been placed there (John 20:1–10).

8. The "stigmata" (crucifixion scars) shows it was the same body (Luke 24:39; John 20:25–28).

9. Jesus stated that the body raised would be the same body as the one that died (John 2:19–22, notice "it").

10. Jesus' body did not see corruption after death (Acts 2:31).

11. Paul's "seed" comparison shows it's the same body (see 1 Corinthians 15:35–44, notice pronouns "it" and "this").

Conclusion

The resurrection of Christ is one of the most well-documented historical events of ancient history. The attempts to explain away the empty tomb with other theories have fallen short on several counts, leaving Christ's physical bodily resurrection as the best solution to account for the facts. Not only does the Resurrection match the evidence; it confirms the New Testament's divine authority of Jesus' message of forgiveness, His claim to be divine, and His miraculous and sinless life. The many appearances of Christ in His physical resurrection body provide ample proof that Jesus rose from the dead as the Bible records. To deny the Resurrection event, an event based on abundant documentation and credible eyewitness testimony, would require contradictory eyewitness reports or the untenable position that eyewitness reports can't be relied upon.

Review

1. Why is the resurrection of Jesus important to defend?

_____

_____

_____

_____

2. How does a resurrection differ from a resuscitation?

_____

_____

_____

_____

3. What kind of characteristics will be present in a resurrected body? (See 1 Corinthians 15.)_____

_____

_____

_____

_____

4. What evidences give us good reason to believe Jesus actually rose from the dead?_____

_____

_____
_____
_____
_____

5. What are the problems with the theory that says Jesus fainted and later revived?_____
_____
_____
_____

6. Was Jesus' resurrected body material or immaterial? How do you know? _____
_____
_____
_____

7. List seven reasons why Christians believe Jesus' body was material.

(1)_____
_____

(2)_____
_____

(3)_____
_____

(4)_____
_____

(5)_____
_____

(6)_____
_____

(7)_____
_____

CHAPTER 12

Is the Bible the Word of God?

Scenario

It is Wednesday night at the Bible study meeting at the church. Peter, Jennifer, Jordan, and Sarah are all there. The youth pastor has just completed reading a chapter from the Book of Acts.

Jordan: Who wrote the Book of Acts?

Peter: Most people think that Luke wrote it.

Jordan: Why then do Christians call Acts the Word of God?

Peter: Because God authored the Bible and He used humans to write it.

Sarah: Well, Peter, it just seems that the Bible should have all kinds of mistakes in it because humans were involved.

Jordan: And there are all these books divided into two Testaments. Were they written by a bunch of writers at different times?

Jennifer: That's what we learned last time.

Jordan: I just can't figure out how there are not loads of mistakes and conflicting stories.

Peter: But there aren't any.

Sarah: Why?

Peter: Because the Bible itself is a miracle. The writers were inspired by God, so the Bible is the Word of God. As a result, there can be no mistakes if the Bible consists of the inspired words of a perfect and all-knowing being.

Questions

- Do you believe in the Bible?
- Did the Bible come from God?
- Does the Bible have a special supernatural power?

Purpose

To show the student that the Bible, while written by human authors, has a divine origin

Goal

To understand the reasons why Christians believe the Bible is without error and is the authoritative Word of God

In this chapter we will learn

- that the English word *Bible* comes from the Greek word *biblos,* which means "book" or "roll."
- that the *theme* of the Bible is all about Jesus—by way of *anticipation* in the Old Testament and *realization* in the New Testament.
- that Jesus *confirmed* the Old Testament and *promised* the New Testament.
- that God used people to write the Bible through a process called "inspiration." This process guarantees the Bible is free of error.
- what the Bible has to *say* about its own origin.

The Bible is a unique book that has many faces. Some people study it as history, using it to understand past civilizations and events. Others read the Bible for its poetry and set of moral stories. There is a place and purpose for each of these endeavors, but ultimately the Bible is the Word of God. Specifically, it is God's message to a rebelling world on how to return to Him through His Son, Jesus Christ (John 3:16).

So far we have shown that (1) truth is knowable, (2) God exists, (3) He has a purpose and plan for evil, (4) miracles are possible, (5) the New Testament writings can be seen as accurate copies of the originals, (6) Jesus is God, and (7) He demonstrated His divine nature by His sinless and miraculous life, which culminated in His bodily resurrection from the dead. These conclusions were discovered by reason without referring to the Bible as a book from God. The reliability of the New Testament showed us that the documents we have today can be relied upon as accurate copies of the originals writings. This chapter will answer the question as to whether these accurate copies represent the very words of God.

What is the Bible?

The English word *Bible* comes from the Greek word *biblos,* which means "book" or "roll." *Biblos* was the name given to the papyrus reed that grew along the banks of the Nile River in Egypt in the eleventh century B.C.[1] The word *Bible* has been used to refer to the sixty-six books that comprise the total body of Christian Scripture.

Even though the Bible is one book, it is divided into two testaments called the Old and New Testaments. The Old Testament was written mostly in the Hebrew language and contains thirty-nine books, which are divided into four sections:

1. The Pentateuch, Law, or Torah (Genesis to Deuteronomy)
2. The Historical Books (Joshua to Esther)
3. The Poetical Books (Job to Song of Solomon, or Song of Songs)
4. The Prophets (Isaiah to Malachi)

The New Testament was written in the Greek language and contains twenty-seven books that are also arranged in four sections:

1. The Gospels (Matthew to John)
2. The Acts of the Apostles (Acts)
3. The Epistles (Romans to Jude)
4. The Book of Revelation

What is the Bible about?

Some may view the order of the eight sections of the Bible as being unimportant. Nevertheless, the order of arrangement reveals a detailed historical progression of God's plan to save humanity through Jesus Christ. Jesus is the theme of the Bible in all eight sections of the Old and New Testaments (Matthew 5:17; Luke 24:27, 44; John 5:39; Hebrews 10:5–7).[2]

The Old Testament books of the Law lay the foundation for Christ in that they reveal how God chose a people to represent Him (Genesis), redeemed His people from bondage (Exodus), sanctified His people (Leviticus), guided His people through the wilderness (Numbers), and instructed the children of Israel through whom He was going to bless all nations (Genesis 12:1–3). The historical books illustrate how God was preparing the nation for Christ in order to fulfill its mission of bringing forth a Savior. In the poetical books God encouraged His chosen people to aspire for things on high, especially for Christ. Lastly, in the prophetical books the people look forward in expectation to Christ's first and second coming.

The Gospels of the New Testament bring the Old Testament expectations to full bloom in the historic manifestation of Christ. Here the promised Son of God takes on the nature of humanity and comes to the nation with a message of salvation. Each of the Four Gospels emphasizes Christ's manifestation in a unique way: Matthew stresses Christ's sovereignty; Mark emphasizes His ministry to His people; Luke describes His humanity; and John reveals His deity (John 1:1, 14).

After Christ was crucified and rose again, the Book of Acts records the propagation of Christ. It reveals the earliest accounts of Christianity's missionary activity. Jesus said that His disciples should take the gospel to Jerusalem, Judea, Samaria and to the end of the earth (Acts 1:8).

The Epistles give us the interpretation and application of Christ in His person and work. This is the doctrinal section of the New Testament. Paul tells us how we should understand and apply the works and words of Christ to our lives.

The final book of the Bible, Revelation, illustrates how God brings all things to a consummation in Christ. In other words, it tells us of God's glorious future program in summing up all things in Christ (Colossians 2:9; Ephesians 1:10).

When viewed carefully, the Bible and all its sections form a meaningful account of how God's plan to save rebellious humanity has progressively unfolded in the person of Jesus Christ. In the Old Testament there is *anticipation* for Christ to come; in the New Testament there is a *realization* of His very presence.

Is the Bible the Word of God?

We can be sure the Bible is the Word of God because Jesus, who has been shown to be the Son of God, told us so. His claims about the Bible are based on His authority as God, which was demonstrated to us through His sinless and miraculous life (chap. 10) and His resurrection from the dead (chap. 11). Jesus *confirmed* the authority of the Old Testament and *promised* the New Testament.

What Jesus taught about the Old Testament

Concerning the Old Testament, Jesus taught at least eleven things.

1. It has ultimate authority (Matthew 22:43).
2. It is reliable and trustworthy (Matthew 26:54).
3. It is the final word (Matthew 4:4, 7, 10).
4. It is sufficient and without lack (Luke 16:31).
5. It is indestructible (Matthew 5:17–18; John 10:35).
6. It is unified in its message (Luke 24:27, 44; John 5:39).
7. It is clear in its central message (Luke 24:27).
8. It is historically accurate (Matthew 12:40).
9. It is scientifically factual (Matthew 19:2–5).
10. It is *without error* (inerrant) (Matthew 22:29; John 3:12; 11:17).
11. It is *unbreakable* (infallible) in its truth claim (John 10:35; Luke 16:17).

On various occasions during Jesus' earthly ministry, He spoke of the historical nature of the Bible by mentioning such events as Jonah (Matthew 12:40), the days of Noah (Matthew 24), the prophet Daniel (Matthew 24), and the creation of Adam and Eve (Matthew 19:2–5).

He also spoke of the authority and finality of Scripture as He used the often repeated phrase "It is written" when He defended Himself against the temptations of Satan (Matthew 4:4, 7, 10). Jesus called the Scriptures the "Word" of God and "Scripture" on several occasions (John 10:35; Mark 12:10; John 5:39; 17:17). The phrases "Scripture says" and "God says" appear some thirty-eight hundred times in the Bible and are used interchangeably when referring to the Word of God.

What Scripture Says God Says

God said . . .[3]	Scripture said . . .
Genesis 12:1–3	Galatians 3:8
Exodus 9:13–16	Romans 9:17

Scripture said . . .	God said . . .
Genesis 2:24	Matthew 19:4–5
Psalm 2:1	Acts 4:24–25
Psalm 97:7	Hebrews 1:6

Jesus promised the New Testament

Since Jesus didn't write any books and the New Testament hadn't been written during Jesus' lifetime, He promised the twelve disciples that the Holy Spirit would teach and "bring to remembrance" all that He had spoken to them (John 14:25–26). Jesus went on to say, "When He, the Spirit of truth, has come, He will guide you into all truth; for He will not speak on His own authority, but whatever He hears He will speak; and He will tell you what things to come" (John 16:13). The apostles understood these statements to mean that additional truths would soon be given so the church could be established. This era of revelation spanned approximately sixty-five years, from the outpouring of the Holy Spirit on the church (Acts 2:1ff.) until the death of the final apostle, John (about A.D. 100).

If Jesus is God, and He spoke the truth that the Old Testament was the Word of God and the New Testament would be written solely by His apostles and prophets, then our Bible is proven to be from God. In other words, the only way to disprove what Jesus said about the Bible is to show that Jesus isn't God.

Did God or man write the Bible?

The process by which the Bible was written is called "inspiration." The term comes from 2 Timothy 3:16 where Paul says, "All Scripture is given by *inspiration* of God, and is profitable for doctrine, for reproof, for correction, for instruction in righteousness, that the man of God may be complete, thoroughly equipped for every good work" (emphasis added). Literally, the word means "God-breathed." That is to say, God is the source or originator or cause of Scripture.

Paul's statement doesn't limit inspiration only to the Old Testament; it also applies to the New Testament. This can be confirmed by a reading of 1 Timothy 5:18, which says, "For the Scripture says, 'You shall not muzzle an ox while it treads out the grain,' and, 'The laborer is worthy of his wages.'" Notice that Paul quotes Deuteronomy 25:4 and Luke 10:7 and calls both passages "Scripture," placing both passages on the same inspired level with the rest of Scripture. The apostles also recognized the New Testament as "Scripture." This is seen in Peter's statement that places Paul's letters (epistles) on the level of "Scripture" (see 2 Peter 3:16). At the time Peter and Paul made their statements, most of the New Testament had already been written, with the exception of 2 Peter, Hebrews, Jude, and the apostle John's writings.

God used human instruments (apostles and prophets) to write the words of Scripture (2 Peter 1:19–21). This doesn't mean that the individual characteristics of each writer were removed. On the contrary, they are kept and used in their own individual way. This is why each book of the Bible reflects the unique style of the writer. God fully incorporated human aspects in Scripture such as the following:

1. Different *human literary styles* reflect the different authors.
2. Different *human interests* and needs are discussed (2 Timothy 4:13).
3. Different *human perspectives* (Gospels) present the life of Christ.
4. Different *human terms* are used to speak of God (Isaiah 53:1; anthropomorphisms [*anthropos* = man, *morphe* = form]).
5. Different *human languages* are used (Hebrew, Aramaic, Greek).
6. It utilizes *human memory* (1 Corinthians 1:15–16).
7. It speaks from *human perspective* (Joshua 10:12–13).

It is important to remember that even though God allowed human participation in the writing of Scripture (1 Corinthians 2:13), it is still without error because God gave the revelation and oversaw the writing. In other words, we have the Word of God written by men of God. The logic behind the inerrancy (without error) of the Bible is as follows:

> The Bible is the Word of God.
> God can't err.
> Therefore, the Bible can't err.

The objection is sometimes raised: "The Bible isn't the inerrant Word of God; it was written by fallible men." *First,* we ought to remember to point out the two different roles occupied by God and man. God was the author who oversaw it and man was the writer of Scripture who recorded it. Divine inspiration was the necessary insurance to preserve the purity and inerrancy of the Word of God. *Second,* humans don't always err, only sometimes. This means that the writers of the Bible could have written the Scriptures without error. Further, the apostle Peter tells us the writers of Scripture were carried along by the Holy Spirit (2 Peter 1:21).

What does the Bible claim about itself?

Just as a person is allowed to testify in a court of law on his own behalf, so also is the Bible allowed to speak on its own behalf. Several unique claims within the Bible itself witness to its divine origin.

1. Paul claimed that the things he was writing were indeed the Lord's commandments (1 Corinthians 14:37) and were accepted by believers (1 Thessalonians 2:13).

2. Peter acknowledged the Word of God as unchangeable and worthy of our obedience (2 Peter 1:16–21).

3. John recognized that his teaching was from God and that to reject it was to reject God (1 John 4:6).

4. All the apostles and prophets who made claims concerning the integrity of Scripture often defended it at great personal sacrifice, even to the point of death (Jeremiah 11:21; Philippians 2:7, 17).

5. Throughout the pages of the Bible, the often repeated phrases "God says," "Scripture says," "The Lord spoke saying," and "thus says the Lord" remind the reader that indeed the Bible is inspired by God (Exodus 14:1; 20:1; Leviticus 4:1; Numbers 4:1; Isaiah 1:10, 24).

6. The unity of the Bible is a powerful testimony to inspiration. Throughout Scripture there exists one harmonious theme without contradiction. This crucial piece of evidence is appreciated when one remembers that the Bible was written by some thirty-five different writers from all walks of life, writing on different controversial subjects over a span of fifteen hundred years on three different continents.

There are other reasons why we believe God inspired the Bible; however, the ones stated thus far should be sufficient to convince an open-minded skeptic. Without claiming these proofs as inescapable evidence, they do, however, give us good reason to believe God wholly inspired the Bible. It is in the inward recesses of the soul that the judge and jury of the evidence presented must make a decision. For those who tend to be indecisive, one is reminded of the words of Peter: "Lord, to whom shall we go? You have the words of eternal life" (John 6:68).

Review

1. What is the meaning of the word *Bible?*

_____

_____

_____

_____

2. In a few sentences, describe what the Bible is about.

_____

_____

_____

_____

3. What role does Jesus occupy in establishing the Bible as the Word of God? _____

_____

_____

_____

_____

4. What does "inspiration" mean? _____

_____

_____

_____

_____

5. How do we know that the books of the New Testament are inspired by God? List two verses in your answer.

_____

_____

_____

_____

6. What role does the Holy Spirit occupy in the inspiration process? List one verse with your answer. _____

_____

_____

_____

_____

7. How does the Bible itself show evidence of inspiration?

_____

_____

_____

_____

CHAPTER 13
Responding with Wisdom

Scenario

After the Bible study session, the four high schoolers are driving home in Peter's car.

Jordan: You know, what? God, Jesus, the Holy Spirit, the Bible—all this is starting to make sense to me.

Sarah: He must love us.

Jennifer: That's right. Jesus is love, and He died to save us.

Peter: He died so we could live in heaven for eternity. And, Jordan, think about the alternative.

Jordan: Pretty grim. I think Sarah and I want to join you guys on Sunday mornings and Wednesday evenings.

Peter: What about the waves on Sunday mornings?

Jordan: I look at it this way, Peter: heaven has got to be more enjoyable than killer six-foot waves. I want to be on an eternal surfari.

Jennifer: That's what my brother dreams about.

Sarah: Do you know where we can get two Bibles that we can read and understand?

Jennifer: Don't you have Bibles at home?

Jordan: I've never seen any. The folks aren't into it.

Peter: I'll ask the youth pastor to get you two Bibles.

Jordan: Sarah, can you imagine how Mom and Dad will react when they find us reading Bibles?

Sarah: I think Mom might like to join us.

Jordan: Yeah, could be. What about Dad? He's always making jokes about closed-minded Christians. Peter, where do I start with him?

Peter: He still surfs, right?

Jordan: Sort of, you know, on an old-fashioned surfboard.

Peter: I know the perfect time—my place about 1:00 on Sunday afternoon when the wind comes onshore and the waves get choppy. Worked for you, didn't it?

Jordan: Amen!

Questions

- How do you react when people attack your faith?
- What do you say to authority figures that are prejudiced against your faith?
- How do you turn an awkward situation into a witnessing event?

Purpose

To be prepared for the intellectual and moral challenges to the Christian faith encountered in the college classroom

Goal

To be equipped with several principles that can be applied with success when challenged with anti-Christian ideas

In this chapter we will learn

- that the college classroom can be an intellectually stimulating place and yet still be antagonistic and prejudiced against Christian ideas.
- that there are several principles that Christians can apply in the classroom to turn a potentially uncontrolled reaction into a controlled action.

What should I expect in college?

Gaining knowledge through a college education is a good thing. Proverbs 1:5 tells us that "a wise man will hear and increase learning." Most colleges and universities have formed their programs to provide an atmosphere in which to learn a host of subjects. A professor lecturing on a topic throughout a given semester usually accomplishes this task. Among some of the classes offered are usually history, mathematics, engineering, literature, philosophy, English, science, and sometimes even theology and religion.

At this point you might say, "So far college sounds pretty normal, so what's the big deal?" First, let's understand where the problem isn't. The problem doesn't necessarily exist in the *expression* of ideas that do not agree with Christianity. However, there is a problem with the unfair *assumptions* when expressing ideas against Christianity. But what is an "unfair assumption"? An unfair assumption can also be called a "bias" or a "prejudice." Let's remember, however, that not all bias and prejudices are wrong. For example, most of us have a bias for good and are prejudiced against immoral acts. This bias even extends to our government lawmakers who clearly express a bias in favor of peace, safety, and the right to enjoy life. All rational people have biases.

The question is whether the bias you possess is correct and fairly presented. An unfair bias occurs when professors or classmates treat students unequally or make statements that are couched in false assumptions. The problem of unfair bias can target Christianity as a religion or those who believe Christianity is true. The implicit goal of these prejudices are most often to shape or influence the hearers' minds by intimidation or peer pressure into thinking Christians and/or Christianity is irrational, dumb, unbelievable, intolerable, narrow-minded, archaic, and impossible. Notice the following examples of statements that reflect an unfair bias. Try to detect the unfair assumption.

1. "All rational people know that evolution is true."
2. "All of us in this class believe in the woman's right to choose abortion, right?"
3. "Now that modern man knows miracles are impossible, how do we interpret the myth of the resurrection of Jesus?"
4. "Since all informed people understand that no one possesses the truth, how might we approach our classroom discussions?"
5. "All educated people know that morals are relative."

Most of the above examples contain attacks against the Christian students' rationality or believability of their worldview. That is to say, if you don't believe what is said in the examples, you're considered uninformed, irrational, unintelligent, narrow-minded, and outdated. This seems to be a powerful force since no one wants to be viewed by peers in those undesirable categories, especially in an institution for higher education. Biases can also occur in grading and showing partiality in classroom discussions. The good news is that there are several biblical principles that can be applied in class to ensure the integrity and believability of the Christian worldview.

W-I-S-D-O-M

How do we respond when Christianity is under attack in the classroom? Unfortunately, more often than not, when students are challenged or confronted with a bias or an alternative viewpoint, they react with an emotional outburst of rage. The class is immediately stunned as the student slithers back into his or her seat with the wild-eyed look of a fire-and-brimstone prophet. Even if the student is on the right side of the issue, the manner in which he addresses the issue is also important.

If you find yourself faced with bias in the classroom, six biblical principles can help you respond intelligently without compromising Christianity or your character.[1] These principles can be easily remembered through the acronym W-I-S-D-O-M.

Walk in the Word

By immersing yourself in God's Word, two important things occur. First, you ensure yourself a sober and alert mind by which to discern what is true and false and what is right and wrong. Your spiritual antennas will develop an uncanny characteristic for detecting error (Hebrews 5:11–14). This is because the Bible stands as the ultimate standard by which to judge the most crucial ideas. Paul wrote to Timothy that "all Scripture is given by inspiration of God, and is profitable for doctrine, for reproof, for correction, for instruction in righteousness, that the man of God may be complete, thoroughly equipped for every good work" (2 Timothy 3:16–17).

The second benefit of walking in the Word is that the relationship you have with God through His Word conveys a sanctifying and cleansing effect (Ephesians 5:26; 1 Corinthians 6:11) that keeps you rooted and grounded to the Lord even in an intellectually contaminating environment.

Investigate the issues

Oftentimes we want to react immediately to the attack as it is occurring. And sometimes we should—if we have a knowledgeable response that reflects sound research and not simply the rage of emotion. Yes, our walk with Christ is foundational to a proper response; however, it doesn't excuse us from diligent research and investigative study. The apostle Paul was a perfect example of one who had a well-rounded knowledge of the issues. In Acts 17:16–34, Paul began to witness to the pagan philosophers in Athens when he quoted the words of two pagan poets by saying, "For we are also His offspring." Paul's main purpose for using this quote was to show the philosophers that it is unreasonable to believe that gold, silver, and stone idols are responsible for human existence (17:29). In other words, it doesn't make sense to believe that personal beings (humans) came from impersonal stone idols, or that intelligent (humans) arose from nonintelligent materials such as gold, silver, or stone. Much in the same manner, we as Christians should investigate the issues before responding. The answer to your professor's attack may be found on the internet or printed in a book at your local library. Gather the information and then be ready to apply your research when the next opportunity arises. Don't worry, God will open the doors.

Sit with the Savior

This principle encourages us to spend time with Christ. There is no substitute for a loving relationship with the Creator of the universe when preparing for battle. All of us want to respond to attacks reasonably, so it makes sense to draw close to the One "in whom are hidden all the treasures of wisdom and knowledge" (Colossians 2:3). How do we draw close to Him and make ourselves knowledgeable and wise? Proverbs 1:7 says, "The fear of the LORD is the beginning of knowledge." There is no better foundation on which to build a proper response than getting in touch with the Lord through prayer, worship, and meditation on His Word. There might be something important He wants to say to you during your time with Him.

Delicate demeanor

Some of us distance and bring reproach on ourselves from our classmates and professors unknowingly. It's not done necessarily by *what* we say, but *how* we say it. Our attitudes can be a problem if not checked early. The apostle Peter reminds us that when we give reasons for what we believe, it must be accomplished through "meekness and fear" (1 Peter 3:15) and with gentleness and respect. This is because our attitudes are usually the first thing people notice when we talk with them. Attitudes have the potential to become huge obstacles that could prevent someone from understanding your position on a particular issue, thus preventing a Christian conversion. Moreover, being that the Christian position on issues are usually considered the most intolerant views on campus, other students have a tendency to observe and scrutinize your actions and attitudes more closely. Peter said, "Having a good conscience, that when they defame you as evildoers, those who revile your good conduct in Christ may be ashamed" (1 Peter 3:16). Not only does a good demeanor help give you credibility among your peers, it is a positive representation of Christ.

Demeanor within the classroom also extends to your professor. Even if you have a good answer or viewpoint that refutes a particular issue, nobody likes to lose face or the respect of others, especially in front of the entire class. If the teacher loses face, you've probably lost an opportunity for further discussions about other crucial issues. It may be better to talk with your professor after class or schedule a time to meet in his or her office. How we do something is just as important as what we do.

Oppose obstacles

Rarely do Christian college students complete a semester without experiencing an attack against their faith. When the attack arises, we have two choices: do *nothing* or do *something*. The Bible tells us that we are to respond to questions and attacks of our faith. Peter said, "be ready to give a defense to everyone who asks you a reason for the hope that is in you, with meekness and fear" (1 Peter 3:15). The Bible doesn't stop there. Paul speaks to the Corinthian church about "casting down arguments and every high thing that exalts itself against the knowledge of God, bringing every thought into captivity to the obedience of Christ" (2 Corinthians 10:5). As mentioned before, we want to give informed and polite responses—but does this extend to *all* attacks or controversial issues? No, we must pick our issues wisely; some less important things are better left unaddressed. For example, the issue of whether the Christian church had one thousand or five thousand members after its first year of existence is unimportant and has no bearing on the truthfulness of Christianity and should be avoided. The chances that your peers and professors will be interested in your viewpoint is greatly enhanced if you haven't wasted your words on trivial issues. Issues that should be addressed are the existence of God, the possibility of miracles, the deity of Christ, the historical reliability of Bible, the resurrection, and the creation of the universe. In other words, all the topics mentioned in the previous chapters are foundational to our faith.

Meeting with a mentor

Schedule regular times in a given month to meet with a mentor (2 Timothy 2:2), a mature Christian friend or teacher who is willing to meet with you occasionally to pray for or discuss tough issues that may arise in your studies. You would be surprised how many Christians are on campus, not to mention Christian professors. They can be found through local churches and student newspapers and bulletins. A good mentor can contribute several important components to both your educational and spiritual life while in college. First, your mentor provides needed accountability. Second, they offer leadership by offering their best ideas when you are faced with tough educational or spiritual circumstances. Third, Christian companionship can guard against isolation or loneliness. The general recommendation is that your mentor be of the same gender. Finally, mentors provide good opportunities for a prayer partner.

Conclusion

The Bible commands us to "defend" the faith (Philippians 1:7), but we should not be defensive about it. We should also contend for the faith (Jude 3) without being contentious. We should speak the truth, but it should be spoken *in love* (Ephesians 4:15). We never want to win the argument and lose the soul. Paul urged us to let our "speech always be with grace . . . that you may know how you ought to answer each one" (Colossians 4:6).

Review

1. Describe the difference between fair and unfair assumptions.

_____

_____

_____

_____

_____

_____

_____

2. What does the acronym W-I-S-D-O-M mean?_____

_____

_____

_____

_____

_____

_____

3. How would you respond when an authority figure challenges your faith?_____

_____

_____

_____

_____

_____

4. What topics would be worthwhile to address in class?

_____

_____

_____

_____

_____

_____

_____

Where Do You Go from Here?

Congratulations! You have completed the basics of apologetics. But what should you do next? The following are several ideas that may help you.

1. There is nothing better than to become more familiar with your Bible. Several terrific passages give examples of how apologetics was accomplished by heroes of the faith: 1 Kings 18:17–40 tells of Elijah's apologetic encounter with the prophets of Baal; Acts 17:16–34 conveys Paul's apologetic response to the Stoic and Epicurean philosophers in Athens; God did apologetics with Moses in Exodus 4:1–9. Then search through the Gospels and discover how Jesus responded to the Pharisees and Sadducees.

2. Continue reading good books on how to defend your faith and win others to Christ. Check the "Recommended Reading" list on the next page.

3. Remember to review the apologetic chapters. Keeping the information fresh in your mind will ensure your readiness to respond when God gives the opportunity.

4. Most importantly, remember why you have learned to defend God's Word. It is a tool to help you defend Christianity and reach others for Christ more effectively.

Recommended Reading

Beckwith, Francis J. and Greg Koukl. *Relativism: Feet Firmly Planted in Mid-Air.* Grand Rapids: Baker Books, 1998.

Behe, Michael J. *Darwin's Black Box.* New York: The Free Press, 1996.

Bloom, Allan. *The Closing of the American Mind.* New York: Simon & Schuster, 1987.

Budziszewski, J. *How to Stay Christian in College.* Colorado Springs: NavPress, 1999.

Cuozzo, Jack. *Buried Alive: The Startling Truth about Neanderthal Man.* Green Forest, Ark.: Master Books, 1998.

Elwell, Walter A. *Evangelical Commentary on the Bible.* Grand Rapids: Baker Books, 1989.

———. *Evangelical Dictionary of Biblical Theology.* Grand Rapids: Baker Books, 1996.

———. *Evangelical Dictionary of Theology.* Grand Rapids: Baker Books, 1984.

———. *Topical Analysis of the Bible.* Grand Rapids: Baker Books, 1991.

Geisler, Norman L. *Baker Encyclopedia of Christian Apologetics.* Grand Rapids: Baker Books, 1999.

———. *Christian Apologetics.* Grand Rapids: Baker Books, 1976.

——— and Abdul Saleeb. *Answering Islam: The Crescent in Light of the Cross.* Grand Rapids: Baker Books, 1993.

——— and Peter Bocchino. *Unshakable Foundations.* Minneapolis: Bethany House Publishers, 2001

———— and Thomas Howe. *When Critics Ask*. Wheaton: Victor Books, 1992.

————. *When Cultists Ask*. Grand Rapids: Baker Books, 1997.

———— and Francis J. Beckwith. *Abortion and Euthanasia: Matters of Life and Death*. Grand Rapids: Baker Books, 1991.

———— and Frank Turek. *Legislating Morality: Is It Wise? Is It Legal? Is It Possible?* Minneapolis: Bethany House Publishers, 1998.

———— and Ronald M. Brooks. *When Skeptics Ask*. Wheaton: Victor Books, 1990.

———— and William E. Nix. *A General Introduction to the Bible: Revised and Expanded Edition*. Chicago: Moody Press, 1986.

———— and William D. Watkins. *Worlds Apart: A Handbook on Worldviews*. Grand Rapids: Baker Books, 1989.

Gish, Duane. *Evolution: The Fossils Say No*. San Diego: Creation Life Publishers, 1981.

Greenleaf, Simon. *The Testimony of the Evangelists*. Grand Rapids: Kregel, 1995.

Groothuis, Douglas. *Truth Decay: Defending Christianity against the Challenges of Post Modernism* (Downers Grove: IVP, 2000).

Habermas, Gary. *The Historical Jesus: Ancient Evidence for the Life of Christ*. Joplin, Mo.: College Press, 1996.

Halverson, Dean, ed. *The Compact Guide to World Religions*. Minneapolis: Bethany House Publishers, 1996.

Hanegraaff, Hank. *The Face That Demonstrates the Farce of Evolution*. Nashville: Word Publishing, 1998.

————. *Resurrection*. Nashville: Word Publishing, 2000.

Heeren, Fred. *Show Me God: What the Message from Space Is Telling Us about God*. Wheeling, Ill.: Searchlight Publications, 1995.

House, H. Wayne. *Charts of Christian Theology and Doctrine*. Grand Rapids: Zondervan, 1992.

————. *Charts of Cults, Sects, & Religious Movements*. Grand Rapids: Zondervan, 2000.

Johnson, Phillip E. *Defeating Darwinism by Opening Minds*. Downers Grove: InterVarsity Press, 1997.

————. *Darwin on Trial*. Downers Grove: InterVarsity Press, 1993.

Kole, André and Jerry MacGregor. *Mind Games: Exposing Today's Psychics, Frauds, and False Spiritual Phenomena*. Eugene, Ore.: Harvest House, 1998.

Lewis, C. S. *Mere Christianity*. New York: Macmillan, 1965.

————. *Miracles*. New York: Simon & Schuster, 1975.

————. *The Problem of Pain*. New York: Macmillan, 1940.

————. *The Great Divorce*. New York: Simon & Schuster, 1974.

————. *The Abolition of Man*. New York: Simon & Schuster, 1975.

Little, Paul. *Know Why You Believe*. Downers Grove: InterVarsity Press, 1988.

Lubenow, Marvin L. *Bones of Contention: A Creationist Assessment of Human Fossils*. Grand Rapids: Baker, 1992.

McDowell, Josh. *The New Evidence That Demands a Verdict*. Nashville: Thomas Nelson Publishers, 1999.

Moreland, J. P. *Loving God with All Your Mind*. Colorado Springs: NavPress, 1997.

————. *Scaling the Secular City: A Defense of Christianity*. Grand Rapids: Baker, 1987.

Noebel, David. *Understanding the Times*. Eugene, Ore.: Harvest House Publishers, 1991.

Schwarz, John. *The Compact Guide to the Christian Faith*. Minneapolis: Bethany House Publishers, 1998.

Stewart, Don. *The Bible and Science: Are They in Conflict?* Spokane: AusAmerica Publishers, 1993.

Wells, Jonathan. *Icons of Evolution*. New York: Regnery, 2000.

Notes

Introduction

1. Adapted from William J. Bennett, *The Index of Leading Cultural Indicators* (New York: Simon & Schuster, 1994).

2. G. Richard Bozarth, "On Keeping God Alive," *American Atheist* (November 1977), 8. Cited in John W. Whitehead and John Conlan, "The Establishment of the Religion of Secular Humanism and Its First Amendment Implications," 10 TEX. TECH L. REV. (1978), 40.

3. *Humanist Manifestos I and II,* Paul Kurtz, ed. (Amherst: Prometheus Books, 1973), 17.

4. Source: Congressional Quarterly. Cited in William Bennett, *The Index of Leading Cultural Indicators* (New York: Simon & Schuster, 1994), 83.

5. J. P. Moreland, *Love Your God with All Your Mind* (Colorado Springs: NavPress, 1997), 28.

6. See George Barna, Research Archives: *Teenagers' Beliefs Moving Farther from the Biblical Perspectives* (October 23, 2000), at www. barna.org.

7. Carl Henry, *The Christian Mindset in a Secular Culture* (Portland: Multnomah, 1984) 145–46, as cited in Moreland, *Love Your God with All Your Mind,* 28.

Chapter 1

1. For more information, see Norman L. Geisler, *Baker's Encyclopedia of Christian Apologetics* (Grand Rapids: Baker Books, 1999), 41–44, 607–608.

2. Ibid., 607.

3. Ibid., 239–243. Also see Norman Geisler and Thomas Howe, *When Critics Ask* (Wheaton: Victor Books, 1992), 526–27.

Chapter 2

1. Norman L. Geisler and Ronald M. Brooks, *When Skeptics Ask* (Wheaton: Victor Books, 1990), 9–14.

Chapter 3

1. This chapter based on "The Nature of Truth" in Norman L. Geisler, *Baker's Encyclopedia of Christian Apologetics* (Grand Rapids: Baker Books, 1999), 741–45.

2. Norman L. Geisler and Ronald M. Brooks, *When Skeptics Ask* (Wheaton: Victor Books, 1990), 260–63.

3. Ibid., 263–65.

4. Allan Bloom, *The Closing of the American Mind: How Higher Education Has Failed Democracy and Impoverished the Souls of Today's Students* (New York: Simon & Schuster, 1987), 25.

Chapter 4

1. See Fred Heeren, *Show Me God: What the Message from Space Is Telling Us about God,* vol. 1 (Wheeling, Ill.: Searchlight Publications, 1995).

2. Ibid., 81, 102–104.

3. See William A. Dembski, *Intelligent Design: The Bridge between Science and Theology* (Downers Grove: IVP, 1999).

4. See Norman L. Geisler, *Baker's Encyclopedia of Christian Apologetics* (Grand Rapids: Baker Books, 1999), 276–83.

5. Richard Dawkins, *The Blind Watchmaker* (New York: W. W. Norton & Co., 1987), 17–18, 116.

6. Michael J. Behe, *Darwin's Black Box: The Biochemical Challenge to Evolution* (New York: The Free Press, 1996), 232.

7. Hugh Ross, *The Fingerprint of God* (Orange, California: Promise Publishing Co., 1991), 130–31.

Chapter 5

1. For an easy-to-understand book that exposes the errors of evolution, see Phillip E. Johnson, *Defeating Darwinism by Opening Minds* (Downers Grove: InterVarsity Press, 1997). For more advanced reading from a non-Christian point of view, see Michael Denton, *Evolution: A Theory in Crisis* (Bethesda: Adler & Adler, 1985).

2. For more information on chemical evolution, also called "prebiological evolution," see Phillip E. Johnson, *Darwin on Trial* (Downers Grove: IVP, 1991), 102–112, 199–200.

3. Charles Darwin, *The Origin of Species,* Great Books Series (New York: Random House, 1993), 232.

4. Michael J. Behe, *Darwin's Black Box: The Biochemical Challenge to Evolution* (New York: The Free Press, 1996).

5. Ibid., 39–48.

6. Richard Dawkins, *The Blind Watchmaker* (New York: W. W. Norton & Co., 1987), 21.

7. Norman L. Geisler, *Baker's Encyclopedia of Christian Apologetics* (Grand Rapids: Baker Books, 1999), 224–28.

8. See Jonathan Wells's excellent book *Icons of Evolution* (N. Y.: Regnery Publishing, 2000).

9. See Duane T. Gish, *Evolution: The Fossils Say No* (San Diego: Creation Life Publishing, 1981).

10. Charles Darwin, *On the Origin of Species* (New York: Random House, Inc., 1993), 227.

11. Stephen J. Gould, "The Return of Hopeful Monsters," *Natural History* 86, no. 6 (June 1977): 24.

12. Stephen J. Gould, "Evolution's Erratic Pace," *Natural History* 86, no. 5 (May 1977): 14–15.

13. David M. Raup, "Conflicts between Darwin and Paleontology," *Field Museum of Natural History Bulletin* 50, no. 1 (January 1979): 15.

14. Michael Denton, *Evolution: A Theory in Crisis* (Bethesda: Adler & Adler, 1985), 195.

15. Behe, *Darwin's Black Box,* 187.

16. Geisler, *Encyclopedia of Apologetics,* 227–28.

17. See Marvin L. Lubenow, *Bones of Contention: A Creationist Assessment of Human Fossils* (Grand Rapids: Baker, 1992); Duane T. Gish, *Evolution: The Fossils Say No* (San Diego: Creation Life Publishers, 1981), 75–94, 125–30; Hank Hanegraaff, *The Face That Demonstrates the Farce of Evolution* (Nashville: Word Publishing, 1998).

18. Chart adapted from Geisler & Brooks, *When Skeptics Ask,* 215.

19. Geisler and Anderson, *Origin Science,* 35.

20. *Humanist Manifestos I and II,* Paul Kurtz, ed. (Amherst, N.Y.: Prometheus Books, 1973), 8.

21. Ibid., 13–17.

22. In 1961 the Supreme Court asserted that secular humanism is a religion protected by the first amendment in the case *Torcaso v. Watkins.* Humanist John Dewey concludes his book *A Common Faith* (Yale University Press, 1934), 87, with an explicit and militant call to establish humanism as the "common faith" of humankind. The book ends: "Here are all the elements for a religious faith that shall not be confined to sect, class, or race. Such a faith has always been implicitly the common faith of mankind. It remains to make it explicit and militant."

23. See Norman L. Geisler and J. Kerby Anderson, *Origin Science: A Proposal for the Creation-Evolution Controversy* (Grand Rapids: Baker, 1987).

24. Ibid., 39–40.

25. Robert Jastrow, *God and the Astronomers,* 2nd ed. (New York and London: W. W. Norton & Company, 1992), 107.

Chapter 7

1. Norman L. Geisler and Ronald M. Brooks, *When Skeptics Ask* (Wheaton: Victor Books, 1990), 60–61.

2. Geisler, *Encyclopedia of Apologetics,* 219–24.

3. Norman L. Geisler, *Roots of Evil* (Waco: Word Publishing, 1989), chaps. 4–5.

Chapter 8

1. Norman L. Geisler, *Miracles and the Modern Mind: A Defense of Biblical Miracles* (Grand Rapids: Baker Books, 1992), 14.

2. To expose psychics, frauds, and false spiritual phenomena, see André Kole and Jerry MacGregor, *Mind Games* (Eugene, Ore.: Harvest House, 1998).

3. Norman L Geisler, *Signs and Wonders* (Wheaton: Tyndale House, 1988), 152–54.

4. Geisler, *Signs and Wonders,* 73.

5. For a complete exposition on miracles, see Norman L. Geisler, *Baker's Encyclopedia of Christian Apologetics* (Grand Rapids: Baker Books, 1999), 449–468.

6. Ibid., 458.

7. For more advanced reading, see *In Defense of Miracles: A Comprehensive Case of God's Action in History,* R. Douglas Geivett and Gary Habermas, eds. (Downers Grove: InterVarsity Press, 1997) and C. S. Lewis, *Miracles* (New York: Simon & Schuster, 1975).

Chapter 9

1. Tacitus, *The Annals of Imperial Rome,* rev. ed., Michael Grant, translator (London and New York: Penguin Books, 1989), 365. For more information on evidence for the life of Jesus, see Gary R. Habermas, *The Historical Jesus: Ancient Evidence for the Life of Christ* (Joplin, Mo.: College Press, 1996).

2. Suetonius, The Twelve Caesars, rev. ed., Michael Grant, translator (London and New York: Penguin Books, 1989), 202, 221.

3. A. N. Sherwin-White, *Roman Law and Roman Society in the New Testament* (Grand Rapids: Baker Books, 1963), 189.

4. Colin J. Hemer, *The Book of Acts in the Setting of Hellenistic History* (Winona Lake, Ind.: Eisenbrauns, 1990), 376–382.

5. Ibid., 108–158

6. Nelson Glueck, *Rivers in the Desert: A History of the Negev* (New York: Farrar, Strauss, & Cudahy, 1959), 31.

7. Millar Burrows, *What Mean These Stones?* (New Haven: American Schools of Oriental Research, 1941), 1.

8. W. M. Ramsey, *The Bearing of Recent Discovery on the Trustworthiness of the New Testament* (Grand Rapids: Baker Books, 1953), 222, in Josh McDowell, *The New Evidence That Demands a Verdict* (Nashville: Thomas Nelson Publishers, 1999), 63.

9. William F. Albright, *The Biblical Period from Abraham to Ezra* (New York: Harper & Row, 1960), 1–2, in McDowell, *Evidence: Vol. I,* 67.

10. See André Kole and Jerry MacGregor, *Mind Games* (Eugene, Ore.: Harvest House, 1998), 37–52, and Norman L Geisler, *Signs and Wonders* (Wheaton: Tyndale House, 1988), 52–54.

Chapter 10

1. For more information on the deity of Christ before His birth, see Ron Rhodes, *Christ before the Manger: The Life and Times of the Preincarnate Christ* (Grand Rapids: Baker Books, 1992).

2. For more fulfilled prophecy, see Rhodes, *Christ before the Manger,* 235–36.

3. Ron Rhodes, *Reasoning from the Scriptures with the Jehovah's Witnesses* (Eugene: Harvest House, 1993), 135–36.

4. Norman L. Geisler and Thomas Howe, *When Critics Ask* (Wheaton: Victor Books, 1992), 420.

5. Ibid., 472.

6. Norman L. Geisler and Ronald M. Brooks, *When Skeptics Ask* (Wheaton: Victor Books, 1990), 113.

7. See Simon Greenleaf, *The Testimony of the Evangelists* (Grand Rapids: Kregel, 1995).

Chapter 11

1. Norman L. Geisler, *Baker's Encyclopedia of Christian Apologetics* (Grand Rapids: Baker Books, 1999), 644–670.

2. For more information on problems with hypnotism and past life regression, see André Kole and Jerry MacGregor, *Mind Games* (Eugene, Ore.: Harvest House, 1998), 141–50.

3. See Norman L. Geisler, *The Battle for the Resurrection,* updated ed. (Nashville, Thomas Nelson Publishers, 1992), 66–86.

4. William D. Edwards, M.D., et. al. "On the Physical Death of Jesus Christ," *Journal of the American Medical Society* 255:11 (21 March 1986), 1463.

5. For more information regarding non-Christian testimony concerning Christ, see F. F. Bruce, *Jesus and Christian Origins Outside the New Testament* (Grand Rapids: Eerdmans, 1974).

6. Tacitus, *Annals of Imperial Rome,* trans. by Michael Grant (New York: Penguin Classics, 1989), 365.

7. Flavius Josephus, *The Complete Works of Josephus,* trans. by William Whiston (Grand Rapids: Kregel, 1981), 379.

8. Quoted from Gary R. Habermas, *The Historical Jesus: Ancient Evidence for the Life of Christ* (Joplin: College Press, 1996), 203, who quoted from the reading in *The Babylonian Talmud,* trans. by I. Epstein (London: Socino, 1935), vol. III *Sanhedrin* 43a, 281. Also see Galatian 3:13 and Luke 23:39 for the usage of the word *hanged.* It can refer to crucifixion.

9. Lucian, *The Death of Peregrine,* 11–13, in *The Works of Lucian of Samosata,* trans. H. W. Fowler and F. G. Fowler, vol. 4 (Oxford: Clarendon, 1949).

10. For a refutation of this theory see Frank Morrison, *Who Moved the Stone?* (Grand Rapids: Zondervan, 1978), 97ff.

11. For advanced reading on this topic, see Robert H. Gundry, *Sōma in Biblical Theology* (Grand Rapids: Zondervan, 1987).

Chapter 12

1. See Norman L. Geisler and William E. Nix, *A General Introduction to the Bible: Revised and Expanded Edition* (Chicago: Moody Press, 1986), 21.

2. Ibid., 27–29.

3. Ibid., 51.

Chapter 13

1. See J. Budziszewski, *How to Stay Christian in College: An Interactive Guide to Keeping the Faith* (Colorado Springs: NavPress, 1999), 119–28.